The New Federalism

The New Federalism

SECOND EDITION

Michael D. Reagan

John G. Sanzone

New York   Oxford
OXFORD UNIVERSITY PRESS
1981

Copyright © 1972, 1981 by Oxford University Press, Inc.

Library of Congress Cataloging in Publication Data

Reagan, Michael D
  The new federalism.

  Bibliography: p.
  Includes index.
    1. Intergovernmental fiscal relations—United States.
  2. Grants-in-aid—United States.   I. Sanzone, John G.,
  joint author.   II. Title.
  HJ275.R3   1981   336.1′85   80–12560
  ISBN 0–19–502772–8

To Celeste
To Janice and Stephanie Ann

Preface to the New Edition

In this edition, we have added a chapter on the important new development of block grants, modified the conceptualization to reflect new thinking in the field, and have brought the entire text up to date on the basis of teaching experience and developments in intergovernmental relationships.

Riverside, California   M.D.R.
Chico, California   J.G.S.
September 1980

Contents

I

Prologue

1

Is Federalism Dead?

Federalism—old style—is dead. Yet federalism—new style —is alive and well and living in the United States. Its name is *intergovernmental relations*.

Old-style federalism is a legal concept, emphasizing a constitutional division of authority and functions between a national government and state governments, with both levels having received their powers independently of each other from a third source—the people. New-style federalism is a political and pragmatic concept, stressing the actual interdependence and sharing of functions between Washington and the states and focusing on the leverage that each actor is able to exert on the other.

Conventional federalism is a static notion. It pictures the relationship between the national government and the states as something fixed for all time by the founding fathers in 1787. The modern notion of federalism, in keeping with the more realistic approach of present-day political analysis, is dynamic; it pictures the intergovernmental relationship as one of constant change in response to social and economic forces as well as to such significant political factors as the party and electoral systems. In formal terms, constitutional divisions are affected only by constitutional amendment. In actual political practice, we have long recognized that Supreme Court decisions, congressional legislation, political custom, and advances in the technology of communications and transportation can all create de facto changes in constitutional provisions. The wording of the Constitution is sufficiently broad to cover a variety of situations; thus the form can remain constant while the content changes radically. This is, in fact, what has happened to federalism.

Finally, we have been accustomed to thinking of federalism as an abstract feature of governmental structure. We need to begin thinking of it as a policy determinant. That is, we need to consider its impact upon the day-by-day operations and concrete activities of government—and the reciprocal impact of expanding governmental activities upon the structural relationship between the levels.

The New Federalism is better referred to as intergovernmental relations both because the phrase alerts us to the changed meaning of the concept and because the cutting edge of federalism lies in the actual (particularly administrative) relationships between the levels of government as they share in the performance of expanding governmental functions. It no longer makes sense to conceptualize federalism as a wall separating the national and state levels of government.

This sharing of functions is most clearly and dramatically seen in the explosive growth of federal grants-in-aid. Such grants—sums of money given by the federal government to lower levels of government in order to finance the performance of specified functions—were estimated at over $80 billion for fiscal 1981, which is more than double the 1975 figure and ten times the amount in 1960. It is on the system of federal grants—both those for specific programs and the

revenue-sharing funds that recipient governments themselves decide how to spend—that this book concentrates, in
order to present a realistic picture of the New Federalism
as we approach the two hundredth anniversary of the writing
of the Constitution.

The sacred triad of American government has always consisted of separation of powers, federalism, and judicial review. In popular usage, each of these concepts has developed its own mythology. In the cases of separation of
powers and judicial review, however, political scientists have
long since exploded the myths. For example, the conventional wisdom regarding the Supreme Court was the assertion that the judges only interpreted the law; they did not
make it or change it. This is how the possession of power
by a group of nine men not accountable to the electorate
was traditionally defended. In the past four decades, his-
torians and political analysts of the Court have made it very
clear that the assertion is ridiculous. Such recent landmark
cases as *Brown* v. *Board of Education* (the desegregation
decisions of 1954–1955), the reapportionment cases, and the
Miranda and *Bakke* decisions make it abundantly clear that
the Supreme Court makes law. Similarly, the conventional
wisdom on the separation of powers, which holds that the
President has no legislative role and the legislature no executive role, has been thoroughly discredited by a generation of
research. A leading book on the Presidency now speaks of
separated institutions sharing power. This is the realistic
picture of presidential-congressional relations and it is now
pretty thoroughly embedded in the literature.

Curiously, the revolution in political analysis that has
moved away from the study of institutions in their legal
forms to the study of realistic political forces and the social
forces behind them has not been widely extended to the
study of federalism. Perhaps because political scientists have

seen federalism as a structural boundary within which politics operates, rather than as an operative element within politics, they have not paid it much attention. Major exceptions lie in the writings of Deil S. Wright, William H. Riker, the late Morton Grodzins, and Daniel J. Elazar. Riker has examined the origins and conditions of maintenance of federalism and concludes that a decentralized party system is the essential condition for retaining what he calls "the federal bargain."[1] However, he continues to define federalism in essentially legalistic terms as a matter of dividing decisions between a central government and regional governments in such a way that each has some category of action in which it can make decisions without consulting the other. Grodzins and Elazar have made an extremely significant contribution by emphasizing the very extensive degree to which the federal and state governments share in decision making regarding the same functions of government, rather than dividing governmental functions so that each level has its own separate area of action.[2] As Grodzins put it in a now-famous essay,[3] American federalism is not like a layer cake, with each level of government having its own autonomous sphere of decision making; rather, it is like a marble cake, in that decisions regarding a particular function are made at all levels of government, and that all levels typically cooperate in implementing public policies.

An interesting example of such shared governance lies in the unusual provision in national legislation regarding automobile pollution emission standards, which permits the state of California to set an antipollution standard that is more stringent than the one mandated by the federal government for the rest of the states. Another example—a longstanding one—is that of cooperative agricultural extension, which is funded both by federal and state governments through the land-grant college system. Yet a third example

6

would be the Elementary and Secondary Education Act of 1965, which—by holding out the carrot of federal funds in specific categories—has given the federal government a partial role in determining educational priorities in local school systems. (This would raise all sorts of hackles if the national government tried to do it in a more direct fashion.)

Like Riker, however, Grodzins and Elazar have improved our understanding of relationships between the national and state and local levels of government without focusing directly on the meaning of federalism. Although this creates a gap through which the conventional myths may continue to escape unchallenged, it may have been a wise decision on their part. When one does try to focus on the meaning of federalism, one finds a set of formalistic criteria that may have little real political significance.

That is to say, even when the formal criteria are met, it turns out that we have learned little about the actual distribution of power or functions between the national, state, and local levels of government. The term *federalism* tells us little about the degree of political centralization in a society. The United Kingdom is a unitary state, yet there are important elements of decentralization and regional autonomy. Despite these anomalies, it is the contribution to decentralized political decision making that is usually thought of as federalism's prime value.

The Theory of Federalism

The modern classic on the subject of federalism is a book by a British authority, K. C. Wheare, in which he defines the federal principle as "the method of dividing powers so that the general and regional governments are each, within a sphere, coordinate and independent." The modern concept of federalism, he says, has been determined by the

7

United States, where in law the general and regional authorities (i.e., the national and state governments) "are not subordinate to one another, but coordinate with each other." In a viable federalism, acording to Wheare, neither level of government must be in a position "to override the terms of their agreement about the power and status which each is to enjoy."[4] The Constitution must be supreme over both levels of government. Discussing the prerequisites of federalism, he adds that the constituent units

> must possess sufficient economic resources to support both an independent general government and independent regional governments. It is not enough that the general government should be able to finance itself; it is essential also that the regional governments should be able to do likewise.[5]

As we shall see in some detail, it is exactly the inability of state governments to finance all the services asked by their citizens that has led to the substantial development of federal grants-in-aid, and perhaps now to a true fiscal crisis at the state-local level, especially in the largest cities. As for the proposition that the American states are coordinate with rather than subordinate to the national government, one can only assume that Wheare was not aware of Article VI, Section 2 of the Constitution, which states that national laws are "the supreme Law of the Land . . . any Thing in the Constitution or Laws of any State to the Contrary notwithstanding." By any dictionary, *coordinate* means "equal in rank or importance." This the American states, vis-à-vis the national government, are not. As a matter of political theory, in addition, it seems dubious that there can be a nation in which there is *no* institutionalized final authority.

In addition to, or in place of, Wheare's criterion of coordinate legal status, there are several other formal attributes of federalism commonly set forth in academic discussions of the subject. These include:

1. There is a constitutional division of governmental functions such that each level is autonomous in at least one sphere of action;
2. Each government is final and supreme in its constitutionally assigned area;
3. Both levels act directly on citizens (unlike a confederation, where only the regional units act directly on the citizens while the central government acts only on the regional governments);
4. Both levels derive their powers from the "sovereign" (i.e., the people or the Constitution), rather than from one another;
5. Therefore, neither can change the relationship unilaterally; and, finally,
6. The regional divisions (i.e., states) exist as of their own right.

In formal terms, federalism in modern usage is to be distinguished both from *unitary* states, which are those in which all regional and local authority derives legally from the actions of the central government and can be taken away by that government at its pleasure, and, at the other extreme, from mere *confederations,* in which the central government does not reach individual citizens directly—as under the 1783 Articles of Confederation.

The theory of federalism thus stresses the independence of each level from the other and the idea that the functions of government are divided so that some (e.g., defense) are exclusively the province of the central government while others (e.g., education, police protection) belong exclusively to the regional units. In the states'-rights ideology of federalism in the United States, emphasis has traditionally been placed on two constitutional provisions that are thought to embody the notion of autonomous coordinate entities—the Tenth Amendment and the enumerated powers of the national government contained in Article I, Section 8. The Tenth Amendment states that all powers not delegated to the central government, nor forbidden to the states, "are reserved to the States respectively, or to the people." Article I, Section 8 contains a specific list of powers granted to Congress, such as laying taxes, regulating commerce, coining money, providing an army and navy, and granting copyrights and patents. One strand of popular ideology puts these two segments together and infers that the Tenth Amendment reserves to the states everything not listed in the specific grants of power. A supposedly hard and fast line of demarcation is therefore assumed. This ideology conveniently ignores the so-called "elastic clause," coming at the end of the list of ennumerated powers, which states that Congress may "make all Laws which shall be necessary and proper for carrying into Execution the foregoing Powers."

Broad construction of this clause by the Supreme Court, defining "necessary" as meaning appropriate to the end and not explicitly forbidden, so effectively expanded the range of subjects on which the Congress could act that the Court came in 1941 to see the Tenth Amendment as simply stating a truism, "that all is retained which has not yet been surrendered."[6] What the judicial doctrine (originally expounded by John Marshall, then backed away from for many decades, and now dominant again) establishes is that the distribution of powers and functions made in 1789 is not sacrosanct, that Congress can unilaterally change that distribution within the very broad limits of what the Court will accept as appropriate means to enumerated ends. Thus judicial interpretation effectively jumps over the formal hurdle of constitutional amendment as the supposed only way by which the division of functions between the levels can be altered. Since the Supreme Court is an instrument of the national government, and the Constitution is—in a famous phrase—"what the judges say it is," the net effect of judicial review is to permit one instrument of the national government to alter the terms of the federal arrangement unilaterally—despite the text books. Because the Tenth Amendment has no independent power to foreclose expansions of federal activities under the necessary and proper clause, there is no constitutionally binding permanent division of authority between the national and state governments in the United States.

There are some areas of state action into which the national government has, as a matter of policy, not moved. The law of domestic relations is state law. We do not have national legislation on marriage and divorce—except that polygamy is forbidden. Most of the ordinary legislation affecting property and contracts in business generally is state rather than national. Since the "constitutional revolution" of the mid-1930s, however, it is perfectly clear that the national government has the authority under the commerce clause to supersede state business law wherever it finds such action to be necessary, for example, in federal occupational health and safety regulations. While the national government has refrained from pushing its constitutional power as far as it presently could under the elastic clause and under the power to tax and spend,[7] that is a different question from its *legal* ability to supersede state decision making.

It would appear that the only aspect of state government that is beyond the reach of Washington is the very existence of the states with their present boundaries, for the Constitution (Article IV, Section 3) provides that no state may have its boundary changed without its consent. Even the normal processes of constitutional amendment are not legally able to disband a state without its own consent. The governmental structure of the states would seem to be generally a question for self-determination, though even here there is a possibility of national intervention under the clause (Article IV, Section 4) of the Constitution that guarantees to each state "a Republican Form of Government."

The ability of the national government to act in every subject matter area should not, however, be taken to mean that the states have been reduced to nonentities. Although the national government has used its broadened constitutional authority of the past 40 years to take upon itself many burdens with regard to education, health, public welfare, and environmental protection—all areas once thought to lie within the reserved jurisdiction of the states—its entry into these areas has made it a partner with the states rather than a substitute for them. Thus a contemporary British observer, M. J. C. Vile, writes that "the foremost characteristic of American federalism . . . is the *inter*dependence of federal and state governments, not their mutual independence," and that "modern American federalism is characterized more by the extent and importance of [an] area of concurrent power, than by anything else."[8] Federal grants-in-aid represent the most significant means by which the national government presently exercises its concurrent powers with the states. We have not in recent years had much of an extension of domestic programs run *directly* by the national government, but we have had a great extension of programs operated by states and localities with federal funds and with varying (though sometimes very substantial) degrees of federal policy control.

The strictest forms of federal control, constituting the highest degree of federal "intervention," do not consist of federal programs replacing national or state activities.

Rather, they consist of federal administrative actions, legislation, and court decisions that impose national standards in areas where the previously prevailing community standards were those of the respective states or towns. The most noticeable of these interventions are, of course, those involving civil rights and civil liberties. Decisions by the Supreme Court outlawing racial segregation in public facilities, the congressional civil rights acts of 1957 and several succeeding years, and executive orders from the President outlawing discrimination in federal employment—which includes federally funded employment through private business contractors—are all examples of national actions taken to make the Fourteenth Amendment to the Constitution a living reality.

Similarly, a string of Supreme Court decisions strengthening the rights of defendants in criminal cases and in police work, and further shoring up First Amendment rights to freedom of speech and expression in such modern forms as the civil rights demonstrations, exemplifies a degree of *national* concern for civil liberties that is undoubtedly greater than would be the concern of many state legislatures or state courts. Citizen participation rights, as reflected in the one man–one vote decision of the Supreme Court and such legislation as the 1965 and 1970 civil rights acts, with their provisions for compulsory federal voting registrars, also constitute an enlarged area of national standards, with some direct national action. But note that with the exception of the federal voting registrars, the form that the federal action takes is that of imposing requirements upon either states or private individuals; it does not entail the expansion of the "federal octopus" in terms of either funds or civil servants.

Thoughtful observers have recently begun using the label *intrusion* to refer to a different kind of federal intervention: General policy requirements attached to most grants, though

13

often quite unrelated to the particular objectives of the grant. Examples include requirements for planning and project coordination; labor and procurement standards; non-discrimination; citizen participation; and relocation assistance. David B. Walker (assistant director of the Advisory Commission on Intergovernmental Relations) has written of such boilerplate provisions that they "are more intricate, more intrusive, and more pervasive than the programmatic strings of the sixties."[9]

Just as government has learned how to manage the economy as decisively as any explicitly socialist system, yet without engaging in nationalization of the ownership or direct management of plants and factories, so also do we find that the national government can interpose the view of a national majority upon reluctant states and localities and can strongly influence the budgetary allocations of state governments through the choices it makes in its own grant-in-aid allocations, all without in any way touching the formal structure of federalism. The bottle may be old, but the wine is new. Because of court decisions, custom, and the changing social structure induced by "pictures in our heads" uniformly distributed across the country through the mass media and through the travels of an astoundingly mobile population, we have now arrived at point in our constitutional history when no sphere of life is beyond the reach of the national government. Since we almost never question the constitutionality of federal acts, the deciding factor becomes one of policy rather than legality. As William Anderson, a close student of the federal system, wrote in 1955,

When Congress considers any new measure . . . it needs to consider carefully whether it is necessary or even desirable to push national action to the limits of national power. In many situations it may be better, as a matter of public policy, to assist and induce the state and local governments to perform the service up to at least a minimum standard.[10]

This is where grants-in-aid play their part: They are the device by which the national government assists and induces state and local governments.

The distance is considerable between federalism conceived as a legal mechanism by which two levels of government are kept at arm's length from one another and governmental functions are neatly parceled out on a "you do this and he will do that" basis, and the idea of federalism as a political dynamic referring to an interdependent and ever-shifting relationship of joint action. In the older perspective, we look upon federalism as a constitutional bulwark against tyranny. Yet Riker argues with some plausibility that the more one believes in freedom, the less one can approve of federalism historically in the United States, where its main use has been racial represssion. The developing modern perspective pragmatically views federalism as simply a way of getting things done more effectively. From the viewpoint of political science, federalism does indeed have great importance in our system—but that importance does not consist of the original need to compromise between thirteen colonial governments and one central government. Rather, it consists of adding an element of great complexity to political analysis, for in our federal context it becomes a matter for empirical investigation (and reinvestigation because of change) to determine who holds the balance of power and the more influential leverage regarding what each level of government shall do at any particular moment and with regard to any particular subject. In a unitary state, there is less doubt regarding where power lies.

The Textbook Picture

It is not easy to wrench our perspective out of its accustomed angle and refocus it into a better fit with reality. The difficulty is plain if one looks at some of the basic textbooks in American government. Although the average textbook characterization of federalism is more realistic today than when the literature was surveyed for the first edition of this book almost a decade ago, many texts even now state the formal principles of federalism with a straight face, as it were, and then discuss cooperative shared functions or an actual change in the national-state balance of power without connecting the discussion back to their descriptions of the federalist principle.

Several inconsistencies or contradictions develop as a result of this bifurcated treatment, for some of the realistic statements about intergovernmental relations clearly violate what the textbooks have presented as the definition of federalism in America. For example, a widely used book whose third edition was published in 1975 states that American federalism is a system in which "the central government has no legal authority to determine, alter, or abolish the power of the states." On the very next page, however, the authors explain that although Congress could not outlaw billboards on highways because that is not among the enumerated powers, it can provide financial grants-in-aid to the states to build highways "and then pass a law threatening to withdraw financial aid if the states do not outlaw billboards themselves. Thus, the federal government can indirectly enforce its decisions in such areas as highways and billboard regulations."[11] Are the two pages not substantially inconsistent?

A 1978 text describes what the founding fathers created as a federal system and cites three conditions: that at least two levels of government exist with the same territorial and population jurisdiction; that each of these levels "must be autonomous in some specific way"; and that a provision exists to "keep one layer from eventually dominating the other."[12] A few pages later, the same book describes how the Supreme Court drastically altered the federal-state relationship over the years. The book does not explain whether or not these drastic alterations have left federalism intact.

Yet a third text defines federalism as a system that rests on a "divided sovereignty," with national and state governments each controlling "some portion of political power independent of the other's authority." After that very legalistic definition, the author goes on to explain that the reality is quite a different matter and concludes that federalism is essentially a system of government "based on feelings of national community while allowing grassroots ties, sentiments, and loyalties to prosper consistent with" a national sense of values.[13] If we think of a theory as a scientific statement of causal relationships rather than an expression of wishful thinking, then realistic descriptions of the complex relationship between the national and state governments should mean that the theory of federalism is demolished. A theory is not the same thing as an ideal and cannot reasonably be used to explain a basic dimension of a system if the kind of autonomy and power balance called for by the theory simply do not exist.

Our ability to avoid the implications of our empirical descriptions is amazing. Let's just give a final example of this kind. One of the most respected and widely used American government texts of the last quarter century is that of Burns, Peltason, and Cronin. The 1978 edition of this book, *Government by the People*, states what it calls the "formal constitutional framework of our federal system": The national government has only those powers, with one important exception, delegated to it by the Constitution. The states have all the powers not delegated to the central government except those denied them by the Constitution. The authors stress that the national government "must not exercise its powers in such a way as to interfere substantially with the ability of the states to perform their responsibilities," and they cite a 1976 Supreme Court case *(National League of Cities* v. *Usery)* which did restrain national action relative to an extension of the federal minimum wage provisions to state and local government employees. On the other hand, the same authors describe the "tremendous expansion of federal functions" that they feel has taken place as a result of the war power, the power over interstate commerce, and the power to tax and spend for the general welfare. Their summary of the situation is that "we no longer spend so much time debating the *law* of federalism. We now move to the *politics* of federalism. As now interpreted, the Constitution gives us the option to decide *through the political process* [italics added] what we want to do, who is going to pay, and how we are going to get it done."[14] That's a very good explanation, we think, of the present situation. In face of it, why bother to maintain the myth of formal federalism?

It is clear from these examples that federalism needs to be reexamined, not from the viewpoint of abstract conceptualization, but by close description and analysis of the major forms of continuing interaction between the national, state, and local levels of government in the United States. Empirical examination is necessary not only because conceptualization doesn't go far enough, but because we really don't know what the actual story is. While the textbooks all state that federalism and the national-state distribution of power are vital aspects of the American polity, they differ strikingly in their images of what that distribution is and what has happened to us historically.

Here are some of the present textbook characterizations of the distribution of power between the national government and the states:

"The laws of the national government are clearly superior" states a book which then speaks of the "weakness of the states and of local government compared to the government in Washington."[15]

"Governmental activity has been expanding at all levels. . . . Clearly, the basic decisions on the allocation of the limited funds available for grants are made in Washington. . . . Counter balancing these requirements is the fact that primary responsibility for the implementation of federally-aided activities is lodged with state and local officials. . . . The overall impact of federal grants has been to enhance rather than to undermine the capabilities of state and local government."[16]

"The national government has sought to guide the states' use of their power by providing them with money, skills, and information."[17]

"Some part of this almost inevitable federal expansion *has* come at the expense of primary state power. . . . the central government has . . . circumvented, circumscribed, and circumsized [sic] the inherent and exclusive police functionings of states."[18]

Finally, another text says that the general intent of the Framers to decentralize power and to "limit government by balancing competing interests has been realized."[19]

What does this all add up to? We think it essentially demonstrates the bankrupt quality of federalism as an operational concept. If the balance of power betwen the national government and the states is subject to as many different evaluations as these quotations suggest, and if changes in the balance are accomplished from time to time simply by new decisions of the Supreme Court, then two major dimensions of federalism are demonstrated not to exist. One is the notion of permanent autonomy of each level of government from the other, with the corollary of a balance between the two such that neither is distinctly dominant. The other is that whatever the balance may be at a given time, it cannot be changed by unilateral action at either level. Both propositions are today unsupportable. Furthermore—and this is a matter of substantial analytic interest in the study of the development of political science as a discipline—we seem unable even today to devise any concepts by which the extent of federalist principle or the balance of national and state power can be measured empirically. This lack of operationality reduces federalism to the level of mysticism or entrail reading. The primary entrail reader in our system is the Supreme Court. More politely, many of the texts do point out that the Supreme Court continues to be the chief "umpire" of the federalist system. Accordingly, it is time to turn now to a very brief summary of federalist doctrines as they have been enunciated by the Supreme Court over the years, to provide a set of boundaries within which political forces contend.

The Court's Views

Under Chief Justice John Marshall, the Supreme Court stressed national supremacy and implied powers and toally ignored the Tenth Amendment as an independent curb on the powers granted to the national government. The Marshallian precedents are largely the ones operative again today, but in between came a century in which the dominant doctrine of the Court was what the late judicial scholar Edward S. Corwin termed *dual federalism.* In this conception, the distribution of powers between the two levels was seen as fixed and immutable; the states were seen as on an equal level with the national government; and the Tenth Amendment was viewed as carving out an area of exclusive jurisdiction which the supremacy clause could not touch.[20]

Interpretation of the commerce clause was central to explicating the practical meaning of dual federalism, particularly toward the end of the ninetenth century. In one sense, the Court gave great weight to the commerce clause, asserting that it preempted economic regulation from the jurisdiction of the states so that they could not act regarding matters in interstate commerce. At the same time, the Court narrowly defined commerce (so as to exclude manufacturing) and stated that the commerce clause stopped where the Tenth Amendment began. Thus *neither* level of government could act to regulate such matters as wages and hours and child labor. The high (or low) point of this interpretation came in 1918 in *Hammer* v. *Dagenhart*.[21]

In this case, Justice Day's opinion for the majority amended the Tenth Amendment by asserting that to the states "and to the people the powers not *expressly* delegated to the national government are reserved." The word *expressly* is *not* in the amendment, and its inclusion by Day directly contradicts the "necessary and proper clause." The tenor of the Court at that time is inadvertently revealed in the dire fears expressed if the Congress were allowed to regulate child labor:

> If Congress can thus regulate matters intrusted to local authority by prohibition of the movement of commodities in interstate commerce, all freedom of commerce will be at an end, and the power of the states over local matters may be eliminated, and thus our system of government be practically destroyed.

This is the kind of thinking that dominated the Supreme Court until the constitutional revolution of 1937. Since that time, there has been a return to the Marshallian-Hamiltonian principle that where the national government may act at all—and that is almost everywhere under the broad interpretation of implied powers—the so-called reserved powers of the states are no impediment to national action. The Tenth Amendment, as noted earlier, is now seen as stating but a truism, that "all is retained which has not been surrendered." The supremacy clause is back in fashion, and the Court most definitely does not treat the states as coequal sovereigns with the national government. In practical terms, perhaps the strongest indications of what the current interpretation of federalism permits may be seen in such legislation as the Civil Rights Act of 1965, under which federal voting registrars supplanted state officials in several southern states, and in the Supreme Court's decisions in *Baker* v. *Carr* and its sequels, under which the one man–one vote ethic is slowly revolutionizing the composition of state legislatures.

We must note here an unusual "blip" in the post-1937 pattern of judicial construction of the federal balance: in the case of *National League of Cities* v. *Usery* in 1976, the Court (by a 5–4 margin) forbade Congress from extending the minimum wage and maximum hour provisions of the Fair Labor Standards Act to almost all state and municipal employees.[22] Subnational governments had been generally excluded from wage-hour coverage when the act was passed in 1938, although amendments had, by 1966, removed the exemption with respect to employees of state hospitals, institutions, and schools. Writing for the Court, Justice Rehnquist opined in 1976 that "one undoubted attribute of state sovereignty is the States' power to determine the wages which shall be paid to those whom they employ" and that for the national government to supplant "the considered

policy choices of the States' elected officials and administrators as to how they wish to structure pay scales in state
employment" was to interfere impermissibly with "functions
essential to separate and independent existence."

While conceding that federal supremacy does not carry
a right of the national government to destroy a state government, one might still question whether the Court hadn't
rather overstated the impact of applying to the states the
same wage and hour provisions that most private employers
and all of the federal departments had long accommodated
to, as Justice Brennan suggested in his dissent. There he also
stated that he could not recall another instance "when the
reasoning of so many decisions covering so long a span of
time has been discarded in such a roughshod manner."

Does the *Usery* decision mean a return to formal federalism and a restricted scope for national power? Despite the
hopes of the states'-rights advocates, we think not. For one
thing, in the first few years after the opinion was handed
down, a number of lower federal court cases very narrowly
interpreted the *Usery* holding in applying it to similar
matters. For another, the Court itself indicated in a footnote
that it was specifically *not* saying whether the same action
might have been declared legitimate if Congress had rested
it on the spending power or on Section 5 of the Fourteenth
Amendment, rather than on the commerce clause. Thus we
refer to this decision as a "blip" or aberration rather than
as presaging a basic change in constitutional doctrine.

Since the demise of dual federalism, the shorthand phrase
for characterizing the existing phase of nation-state relations
has been *cooperative federalism*. As the words indicate, the
national and state governments work together in the same
areas, sharing functions and therefore power. While the
Federal Bureau of Investigation has its own special roles, it
also runs a training academy for state and local police of-

ficers. U.S. Forest Service personnel cooperate wtih state foresters, U.S. Public Health officers work closely with the state health officers on such matters as communicable diseases or the investigation of water pollution problems, and so on. The general welfare is a matter of *joint* concern these days, with the states actually increasing their own activities at the same time that the federal presence is also growing more noticeable, particularly in financing state activities through grants-in-aid and in selecting particular problems for national priority—e.g., education, health research, the reduction of poverty.

The essential but often overlooked fact about today's cooperative federalism is that it revolves around cooperation in running programs—in doing things—rather than merely in passing statutes. The very nature of modern government is activist and goal-oriented. That is to say, the cutting edge of legislation today does not lie in laws simply prohibiting antisocial behavior by individuals or protecting individual rights. Instead, it consists of statutes that inaugurate administrative programs to advance definite social goals: the elimination of poverty, the beautification of highways, the provision of recreational facilities, the improvement of urban education, the encouragement of scientific research, the provision of public housing for the poor, the revitalization of the cities, the elimination of air and water pollution, the prevention of crime and delinquency, the achievement of equal opportunity for minorities, etc.

Such objectives are not obtained by legislative fiat; they come only (if at all) by continuous programs of social action. For a variety of reasons, effective programs are most often those shared between the national and state levels of government. Thus the currency of the phrase *intergovernmental relations* (even more than cooperative federalism), for the stress today is not on the legal, constitutional positions of the levels of government, but on their practical working relationships. Americans want problems solved. The funds for attacking problems, and often the most effective political impetus, come increasingly from the federal government. But Americans also do not want a "federal octopus"; they do not want local management of programs to be in the hands of federal officials, whether operating locally or—far worse— making particular local decisions from faraway Washington. Hence the compromise of shared functions, permitting both national stimulation and financing and state and local operation of programs to take necessary variations in application into account. The thrust of the New Federalism is to expand the range of modes through which such sharing takes place.

Federalism: An Attitude?

During the administration of President Lyndon B. Johnson, yet another shorthand phrase came into usage: *creative federalism*. This phrase goes beyond cooperative federalism in emphasizing direct federal-city relationships that bypass the states, and—even more significantly—contractual relationships between federal agencies and *nongovernmental* organizations. Community action groups under the war on poverty, containing representatives of the beneficiary groups, illustrate one branch of contractual creative federalism, while the use of private corporations such at Litton Industries and Federal Electric Corporation to run Job Corps centers, or Westinghouse Corporation to devise machinery for programmed instruction, exemplifies the so-called *private federalism* strand.

As long ago as 1954, Don K. Price used the phrase *federalism by contract* to describe the way in which four fifths of the federal government's research and development funds are used to purchase the performance of research by non-federal organizations. While the shift in constitutional doctrine from dual to cooperative federalism made possible the entry of the national government into a number of areas from which it had previously been excluded under narrow interpretations of the Constitution, the shift to creative federalism does not (at least not in all ways) represent a further centralization. Rather, it constitutes the epitome of decentralization in the sense that the federal government not only does not hire its own civil servants to run the programs that the national legislature is funding, but it even reaches below the states to local governments, to semipublic organizations, and to private business firms to administer "its" programs. Moreover, it is not entirely a matter of administrative decentralization; it is also very substantially a question of policy-making decentralization. The exact extent to which grants-in-aid and creative federalism constitute means by which policy making is shared between national and state-local levels will be examined later. It has gone far enough so that one author has written a very provocative book around the thesis that the federal government has in effect lost control of its programs through excessive decentralization of policy making.[23] At this point, one might well ask whether there is anything at all left of the formal, constitutional position of the states in American federalism. The answer is that yes, there is a set of guarantees to the states which provides that the national government shall:

1. guarantee to the states a republican form of government;
2. protect them against invasion and domestic violence;
3. not change a state's boundaries without its consent;
4. maintain equal representation in the Senate for each state.

The existence of the states is therefore guaranteed. Since the theory of a unitary state holds that even the existence of subordinate units is at the will of the central government (as is the case with cities within an American state), this guarantee may be said to constitute the *formal* essence of federalism. Note that this does not imply any particular relationship or division of powers and functions between the states and the national government. It is therefore largely irrelevant to the political controversies over the federal balance, for these concern the *actual* degree of centralization and decentralization and policy-making powers and the *actual* degree of independence or sharing of functions.

On this basis, it can be seen that the legal-juridical approach to federalism is rather inadequate for getting at the really important questions. Just as political freedoms depend far more on the existence of social pluralism and an ideology favorable to them than on formal constitutional guarantees—which can be effective only as a rallying point when these other conditions exist—so also with federalism. The juridical arrangement takes its meaning from and has its vitality or viability determined by the sociological heterogeneity of a society. As William S. Livingston has written,

> The essense of federalism lies not in the institutional or constitutional structure but in the society itself. Federal government is the device by which the federal qualities of the society are articulated and protected. The essential nature of federalism is to be sought for . . . in the forces—economic, social, political, cultural—that have made the outward forms of federalism necessary. Federalism, like most institutional forms, is a solution of or an attempt to solve a certain kind of problem of political organization.[24]

This is a fruitful way of looking at federalism. It is an approach that can help us to address the question of the extent of decentralization of policy making required for effective and rational problem solving in a country like the United

States; for where diversities are important, decentralization is important, and where the culture has been nationalized, then the program decisions and choices of goals can reasonably be nationalized.

Another useful nonjuridical approach to federalism is the relationship of the political-party structure to issues of centralization and decentralization in policy making. There may be a chicken-and-egg question here: Does the constitutional pattern of federalism, under which the states play an important role in the national electoral system, produce the loose, fragmented, decentralized political parties of the United States, or does the American party system produce and sustain the decentralized pattern of policy making that we call federalism? While the two are not mutually exclusive and may indeed be mutually enforcing, David B. Truman has effectively argued that federalism leads to a decentralized party structure, whereas the late Morton Grodzins most convincingly made the case that governmental decentralization is a function of political-party looseness.[25]

The essence of federalism seems to lie in the intangibles. Vile may have defined the crux of the subject when he wrote that "federalism is, perhaps, as much a state of mind as anything else."[26] It is indeed an attitude or habit of mind that leads Americans to place such tremendous emphasis upon the existence of instruments of decentralization in their governmental system. As a pragmatic people, however, Americans also want to get things done. Sometimes this desire comes into conflict with the notion of reliance upon state and local action. Further, our notions of what is appropriately a subject matter for local action and what for national concern change over time. Our age does not see constitutionally fixed distributions of power and functions as the most effective instrumentality for ensuring a simultaneous maximization of effective government and decentralized government. Federalism, like the separation of powers and the institution of judicial review, was a great social invention in 1789. As with the other two basic concepts of the American scheme of government, its meaning in our day must be greatly modified.

While we continue to be a federal system in that both levels of government continue to exist, and not on sufferance from each other, Vile's characterization of the interdependence as the central feature of the system places the emphasis exactly 180 degrees away from the position of states' righters and the conventional ideology. Whether Grodzins is right in saying that the marble cake conception has always characterized the American system, or whether it is more accurate to say that there has been a very considerable shift in this century from a heritage of separation of functions by levels of government toward shared functions, is a question of historical fact that we are not able to settle, although the latter view seems to us to have the better of the argument. The crucial fact is that the functions *are* shared today, whatever may have been the story in the past. And from this flow some further questions:

In the system of shared functions, what is the balance of power? What sources of leverage does each level of government have over the other? To what extent does federal sharing in functions formerly performed entirely by other levels of government constitute policy-making centralization? To what extent, on the other hand, can federal participation through the provision of funds for state and local operations be seen as merely a fiscal relationship without political-power consequences? These questions are closely related to, and cannot be answered apart from, a consideration of the total grant system, including the traditional categorical grants; the general revenue-sharing alternative that President Nixon created in 1972; and the block grants

29

that constitute the most interesting practical compromise in sharing of functions that has occurred in a long time. That consideration has itself a necessary antecedent: a look at the overall pattern of fiscal federalism.

II

The Policy Issues

2

The Crisis of Fiscal Federalism

One of the most succinct and graphic statements of the problem of fiscal federalism was made in 1967 by the former chairman of the Council of Economic Advisers, Professor Walter W. Heller of the University of Minnesota. In arguing for a broad-gauged plan of sharing federal revenues with the states on a no-strings-attached basis, Heller said that the basic reason why this is necessary is that "prosperity gives the national government the affluence and the local governments the effluents."[1] This reference to the "hot" problem of environmental pollution symbolizes the fact that in the United States domestic public services are almost all delivered by state and local governmental units rather than directly by the national government. Social security and veterans' benefits and farmers' subsidies are provided directly by the national government, but the great bulk of public services in the areas of health, education, welfare, housing, highway construction, police protection, parks and recreation, conservation practices, and agricultural extension are provided by state and local units, although all of these (in widely varying degrees) are partially financed by the federal government today. As Heller has written:

A very large part of what we do through government is done through state and local units. They are the ones to whom we usually turn as we seek to maintain and upgrade our educational efforts, improve our physical and mental health, redevelop decaying urban areas, build safer and better highways, overcome air and water pollution, and equip our suburbs with water systems, sewers, roads, parks, schools, and the like. This list is striking partly because each item on it represents either an essential function or a reasonable aspiration of a great and growing society; partly because each item falls squarely within the traditional sphere of state-local operations; and partly because so many items on the list are suffused with a national interest that transcends state and local lines and demands Federal action and support.[2]

It is clear that the areas just mentioned are ones in which we expect state and local governments to provide the services. However, it is not so clear that the quality of services rendered is adequate to our needs or desires. In contrasting the prosperity of our private sector with the relative poverty of our public sector, Professor John Kenneth Galbraith (in his usual quotable manner) by implication expresses a very low estimate of that quality:

The family which takes its mauve and cerise, air-conditioned, power-steered, and power-braked automobile out for a tour passes through cities that are badly paved, made hideous by litter, blighted buildings, billboards, and posts for wires that should long since have been put underground. They pass on into a countryside that has been rendered largely invisible by commercial art. . . . They picnic on exquisitely packaged food from a portable icebox by a polluted stream and go on to spend the night at a park which is a menace to public health and morals. Just before dozing off on an air mattress, beneath a nylon tent, amid the stench of decaying refuse, they may reflect vaguely on the curious unevenness of their blessings. Is this, indeed, the American genius?[3]

Unsatisfactory though the trip may be, one can understand the city family's attempt to escape to the countryside. Riots. Garbage collection strikes. Overloaded telephone circuits. Rat-infested housing. Reading rates up, but libraries forced to close evenings and weekends. Schools that don't educate. Schools that could educate much better if they had funds. Campers outstripping campgrounds. Hospitals overpriced yet understaffed. Clearly, American federalism is a system in crisis.

The Fiscal Crisis

Let us look at the components of that crisis and at the significant trends in governmental finance that both underlie the problem and reflect our thus-far inadequate efforts to deal with it.

The quintessential fact is that alluded to in the quotation that begins this chapter: Affluence lies with the national government, while the effluents are the responsibility of the states and cities. In less colorful language, we suffer from a fiscal mismatch. Although it is much easier for the national government to increase its revenues each year than for state-local governments to do so, the burden of increased demand (and expenses) for public services rests primarily at the doors of the lower jurisdictions. The result is that the ability of state and local governments to meet public demands goes down while their dependence on federal funds and their indebtedness increase, despite substantial revenue increases through courageous tax enactments. Let's spell out these points with some figures that show both trends over time and in the present picture.

1. State-local general revenues, excluding federal aid funds, rose from $15.6 billion in 1948 to $95.4 billion in 1969, and to $200.6 billion in 1976.

2. State-local debt rose from $24 billion to $133.5 billion in the period 1950–1969, and to $277 billion in 1978.
3. The states have been having an even harder time than the localities in paying their expenses out of tax revenues. Between 1964 and 1978, state debt rose four times, to $97 billion, while the local government increase was about 300 percent, to $180 billion.
4. Grants-in-aid, the major kind of federal funds given to the state and local governments, rose from $7 billion in 1960 to $91.8 billion (estimated) for 1982.
5. These federal grants accounted for 33 percent of state-local revenues in 1978.
6. With the help of federal grants and borrowed money, state-local government expenditures rose from $61 billion in 1960 to $335 billion in fiscal 1979. In the same period, the federal-expenditure increase was from $90 billion to $429 billion.[4]

These figures capture the consequences of our fiscal structure. The structure itself can be examined in three parts: the expenditure pattern; the revenue-raising pattern; and the distribution of resources.

On the spending side, we find that the most expensive domestic functions are for the most part the responsibility of the lower levels of government. In terms of direct expenditure (i.e., regardless of which level of government raised the money being spent), taking fiscal 1976 as an example, two thirds of highway expenditures were made by state governments and one third by local governments; and direct expenditures on education were: federal, $7.8 billion; state $2.7 billion; local, $75 billion. Of an all-government expenditure of $49 billion on public welfare, states accounted for $22 billion and localities for almost $12 billion. What domestic functions, if any, are the direct responsibility of the national government? One is natural resources, to a two-thirds extent; others include the postal service and space research, both 100 percent federal; and water transport and air terminals, about three-fourths federal.

If we include indirect expenditure (e.g., federal grants to a state to use in building hospitals, the direct expenditure showing up only as a state item), the picture changes significantly for certain functions. About a third of highway and health and hospital expenditures are then seen as federal, and now more than half of public assistance payments. education, perhaps ideologically the stronghold of local expenditure–local control sentiment, is more federal than expected: One eighth of state-local expenditures are comprised of federal grant funds, in addition to the substantial direct expenditure mentioned above.

What about the other side of the coin—the tax pattern? State-local taxes suffer from triple disabilities: (1) they are inflexible; (2) they are regressive; (3) they cannot provide equal services in all states because they are based on unequal resources. Conversely, federal taxes are much superior, exactly because they are flexible (i.e., responsive to changes in national income); progressive (at least mildly), and provide the only effective means of achieving equalization of services among rich and poor states and cities.

Let us now sketch the major features of the existing tax structure. There are three major categories of taxes, and each is the primary source of revenue for a different level of government:

1. Income taxes—primary source for the federal government, equaling 59 percent of federal tax revenues in 1980;

2. Consumption taxes (especially the general sales tax)—primary source for the states, equaling 52 percent of state tax revenues in 1976;

3. Property taxes—primary source for local governments (and almost the exclusive source for school districts), equaling 81 percent of their fiscal 1976 tax revenues.

Just as each level of government is dominated by a single tax, each type of tax is largely accounted for by one level of government. Thus Washington collected 85 percent of all income taxes (using 1978), while local governments collected 96 percent of all property taxes.

What does it all add up to? Collectively, income taxes (in 1976) accounted for 57 percent of all public tax revenues, consumption taxes for 21 percent, and property levies for 16 percent. Since the national government took the lion's share of the largest revenue producer, it is no surprise to find that it dominates the public revenues picture generally, accounting for 56.5 percent of all public revenues in 1976, with the states at 24.5 and local governments at a mere 19 percent. (Since local governments spend about 29 percent of all direct domestic public expenditures, on the other hand, it is immediately clear that they could not function by reliance upon their own revenue sources; the significance of state and federal grants to localities is manifest.)

These data add up to something else, too: That there has been a drastic centralization in American fiscal federalism, for in 1902 the federal share was not 56.5 but 38 percent; the state share, not 24.5 but 11 percent; and the local share was not 19 but 51 percent! As measured by revenues, the role of the states has clearly not atrophied, but there is a very considerable question of relative financial atrophy at the local level.

Not least among the reasons for federal dominance of the revenue picture is the superior *elasticity* of the income tax, which gives it a considerable political advantage growing out of an economic fact. Let's explain that a little.

Tax elasticity refers to the revenue responsiveness of a tax to changing economic conditions. A tax with low elasticity produces less than a proportionate increase in revenue as taxable incomes rise. In his excellent brief volume on state-local finance, L. L. Ecker-Racz uses the example of the cigarette tax, the yield of which rises only 40 percent as fast as incomes.[5] That is, a 10 percent income increase for a state will produce only a 4-percent cigarette tax revenue increase. State income taxes, on the other hand, have a very high elasticity: A 10-percent increase in economic activity will yield a 15- to 18-percent rise in revenue. At the federal level, the income tax yield runs slightly lower, but is still decidedly elastic. Property taxes have an elasticity of 1.0 (i.e., the yield is proportionate to economic growth), while the general sales tax's elasticity is probably slightly lower than 1.0, since higher-income people save more and spend less, proportionately to income, than lower-income families.

Tax elasticity is an economic fact. Its political implication is that the more a jurisdiction relies on income taxes, with their high elasticity, the larger the revenue increase it can obtain *without having to legislate any increase in tax rates.* The federal government's tax take goes up by $6 or $7 billion annually, with merely average growth in Gross National Product (GNP). Yet the most noticeable changes in federal tax structure in recent years were the 1964 and 1976 income tax *reductions.* The political appeal of increased reliance upon federal funds as an answer to state-local fiscal needs is therefore considerable. Members of city councils and state legislatures are extremely sensitive to the electoral consequences of voting new or increased taxes, but they must also heed public demands for improved and increased services. Because of the latter, they have (often courageously) bitten the bullet in recent years—but not frequently enough or hard enough to prevent a worsening of the state-local balance sheet. The desirable and perhaps only way out of the dilemma, so far as they are concerned, is to pass the financial buck to national congressmen and senators, who have a much pleasanter task than their elected counterparts at the lower levels: Because of automatically increasing federal revenues, thanks to tax elasticity, they need only vote to *spend* the taxpayers' funds in support of state-local services (through grants-in-aid or revenue sharing); they need not bite the tax bullet. This suggests, of course, a self-help route open to courageous state legislatures: if all of them would enact progressive income taxes—only 41 states had done so by 1977—they would soon reap similar benefits for themselves. But they fear to take the plunge, or to increase rates sufficiently to make the tax maximally effective.)

Another major reason for a trend toward greater reliance upon federal revenues to serve the purposes of the entire governmental structure lies in the comparative *regressivity* of state-local taxes. A tax is regressive when it falls proportionately harder on lower-income than on higher-income taxpayers. Although the federal government uses consumption taxes—e.g., on liquor and gasoline—and these are regressive no matter who imposes them, the total impact of federal taxation is progressive because of the predominant reliance upon the progressive income tax. Congressman Henry Reuss has pointed out, in favoring use of federal revenues to support state-local services, that while the federal structure as a whole (prior to recent income tax modifications) took 18 percent of the income of families with incomes below $2000 (showing a need for reform there, too), but 31 percent from families with incomes over $10,000, state-local taxes take only 4 percent from the latter families but 17 percent from those in the $4000–$5000 income bracket.[6]

The property tax in particular is deservedly under attack. Partly this is because it is simply being overworked. It has increased fivefold in the last generation and now accounts for half again as large a percentage of all tax revenues as it did 25 years ago.[7] But also—and people seem to realize this, at least intuitively—real property is a very poor index of ability to pay and no longer is closely related to the kinds of services it is used to provide. Its anachronistic qualities are pointed up in Ecker-Racz's comments:

[In the nineteenth century] when the states granted local school districts the power to tax property, they in fact provided all children with an approximately equal educational opportunity because property value consisted largely of agricultural land and tended to be distributed in proportion to population. Property was then a good prey for people's tax-paying ability, and a tax on property could be levied and collected locally without much difficulty. . . . However, local government no longer limits itself to activities which relate to and benefit property. A large share, typically more than half of local government expenditure, is for services than benefit persons rather than properties. Since we now move about freely, the beneficiaries of today's education, health, or welfare expenditures financed by the property owners of one community are tomorrow likely to be the residents of another community. For this reason it is neither logical nor fair to continue to distribute the cost of education and welfare services in proportion to the assessed value of property to which people happen to hold title.[8]

The lack of relationship between real property values and ability to pay as measured in daily income reached the point of absurdity in California in the mid-seventies, when assessments on homes doubled and tripled in three- and five-year periods. The result of this, and a state budget surplus induced by the economics of inflation interacting with a somewhat progressive state income tax and the politics of a governor, Edmund G. Brown, Jr., who wished to demonstrate his fiscal austerity, was the revolution of Proposition 13—the legislative initiative that now symbolizes nationally the concept of a ceiling on local property taxes. (Just as this was being written, a new initiative was approved by California voters, one which sets a formula limit on the growth of state expenditures.) Ironically, the reaction against the affluence of state and some county governments in California has produced a fiscal backlash that is further hampering the ability of local municipalities to provide services not aided by state or nation but subject to galloping cost inflation.

The third basic characteristic of the American intergovernmental fiscal structure lies in the inequality of resources among the states. Because the taxable capacity of the states varies widely, the tax revenues of state and local governments also vary, and with them the ability of each state to meet the service needs of its people. Unfortunately, with states as with families, those with greatest need for public services tend to be those with lowest resources. Although governments too are subject to "cost of living" differentials from one region to another, the savings obtainable through lower prices in rural states are not as great as the differences in tax capacity. Even by trying harder, the states with lower levels of taxable resources per capita are unable to raise as much revenue as the wealthier states.

Personal income per capita for 1977 ranged all the way from $10,586 in Alaska through $8,061 in Connecticut and $7,911 in California to $5,540 in Alabama and $5,030 in Mississippi. Taking the U.S. average as an index number of 100, state personal income ratios ranged from 79 in Arkansas and 71 in Mississippi to 112 in California and 115 in Connecticut. Although Mississippi makes a greater proportionate effort than does Connecticut (i.e., taxing at higher rates so as to extract a higher percentage of personal incomes), the difference in taxable resources means that the result will not be much better than half as much revenue for the state to use in supplying services to its citizens. The differentials indicated by comparing absolute dollar amounts spent per state on education, public health, or public assistance for families of dependent children are unfairly misleading about those poorer states that, like Avis, "try harder"—but without a chance in the world of becoming No. 1.

Nothing the states can do individually can overcome the differential of resources. "Bootstrapping" only goes so far. The implication is clear: If we decide as a nation that we want a certain level of education, or welfare, or health care for all persons as U.S. citizens, then only the application of the Robin Hood principle through the national government can achieve the goal. That is, only by having Uncle Sam collect more revenues from the wealthier states and distribute more in grants or shared revenues to the poorer states can equalization of services be attained.

Furthermore, resource disparities are at least as great between towns and counties within individual states as between states. The equalization principle therefore also must be applied at the level of "little federalism," by moving the financing of a larger share of essential local government services—such as education—from the local to the state level, with equalization through state grants.

The mid-1971 *Serrano* decision by the California Supreme Court underlined this point. It declared unconstitutional the prevailing pattern of primary reliance upon local property taxes for the financing of public education: The disparity of resources between school districts under this system, said the court, violated the requirement of equal protection of the laws. The range of school finance within the single state of California was illustrated by these figures for 1977–1978: The assessed valuation per average daily high school attendance varied from $430,370 in Taft Union High to $27,444 in Grant Joint Union High district, the statewide median then being $62,045. Expenditures per average daily attendance ranged from under $1,000 to over $4,000, averaging $1,674. For some years after the *Serrano* decision, it was unclear just how the state would adjust its school finance pattern. Then events took over: Proposition 13 so undermined the local tax base for education that the state of California overnight took on a vastly enlarged role through "bailout" legislation. (Not the least of the ironies resulting from the taxpayer initiatives aimed at bringing fiscal power back to the people at the local level is the fact that California school districts and municipal and county governments have become much more subject to state control, through the design of bailout measures, than they were before Proposition 13 "saved them.")

At the end of his thorough review of state-local finances, Ecker-Racz concludes that "the people's prospects for sound public policies improve with the distance between voters and their elected representatives."[9] One corroboration of this sad dictum is the inability of many state and local governments to utilize fully whatever tax capacity they may have. Tax capacity is not automatically translated into tax revenues: Specific legislative action is required. As often as mayors and governors have been impelled to ask for tax increases, there have been an even greater number of cases in which they have either failed to seek increases, or have failed to obtain those sought, in proportion to expanding service needs—otherwise state-local debt would not be increasing so rapidly. Between 1967 and 1977, the per capita increase in state-local taxes ranged from 627 percent in Alaska down to 108 percent in South Dakota, averaging 188 percent. As indicated above, the tax effort among the states varies considerably.

Fiscal capacity is a political as well as an economic concept. Interstate and intercommunity rivalries for business location severely dampen tax-raising proclivities—where such exist at all. Although there is considerable evidence that tax factors are not particularly salient to wealthy individuals or to business firms in locating themselves, it is widely believed (or is at least a fear that no one wants to test) that taxes are decisive in locational decisions. Ecker-Racz effectively sum up both sides of the situation:

Business appears to locate its plants with an eye to the availability of labor, materials, transportation, and space, the accessibility to markets and to other business firms with which frequent contacts are required, and a host of other variables. Increasingly location decisions by business are importantly influenced also by the quality of government services provided to business itself and to the families of the employees. . . .

[On the other hand,] policymakers in state legislatures and city halls yearn for trade and industry and tend to credit the repeated assertions of their business constituents that taxes are influential in business decisions.[10]

So long as this constraining belief exists, no conceivable changes in state-local public finance are likely to solve the intergovernmental revenue problem—even where the resources do exist.

Shared Functions, Shared Expenditures

In the preceding section, we looked mostly at the federal-state-local mix in raising revenues. Now let's look more closely at the spending side. But first, a caveat: Most statistics on governmental expenditure are of direct expenses (i.e., those from a government to its suppliers or its program clientele), and do not reflect intergovernmental transfers of funds (i.e., those granted by a higher level to a lower level to aid in the financing of a service). In such statistics, federal grants do not show up as part of Washington's expenditures, but only as part of state or local direct expenditure. Given the magnitude of grants today (from state to local as well as federal to state levels), this considerably distorts the picture in the direction of minimizing the federal role. We will try to correct for this at appropriate points. On the other hand, the direct expenditure figures are a valid measure to the extent that the significant question may be: Which level supplies the services and meets the citizen's needs rather than: Which level raised the money?

With these qualifications in mind, we will present the facts. In total direct expenditures (including national defense and international relations), we find that over a 60-year period (but in spurts caused by the Great Depression and World War II), the local and federal shares have just about been reversed, with the states playing a smaller in-between role both earlier and now. With national defense taking up over 20 percent of all expenditures, and thus constituting by fare the largest direct expenditure of the national govern-ment, and one of the few functions in which other levels of government do not share significantly, it is not surprising that Washington's share of total public expenditure grew so greatly. Table 1 shows the stages of change.

If we switch our focus to direct domestic-functions expen-ditures, we get a better picture of the three levels of govern-ment in the truly comparable area of consumer activities. Then, as Table 2 illustrates, we find a postwar increase in the federal share, with a steadying trend most recently; an extraordinarily constant state share, and a local decline that has now leveled off.

Considering the absolute increase in local government

THE CRISIS OF FISCAL FEDERALISM

TABLE 1*

PERCENTAGE SHARES OF TOTAL DIRECT PUBLIC EXPENDITURE

	1902	1927	1948	1954	1967	1976
Federal	34	31	62	67	57	53
State	8	12	13	11	16	19
Local	58	57	25	22	27	28

* Source: Frederic C. Mosher and Orville F. Poland, *The Costs of American Governments* (New York: Dodd, Mead, 1964); U.S. Bureau of the Census, *Census of Governments, 1967;* and U.S. Bureau of the Census, *Governmental Finances in 1968–69 and 1976–77.*

from $67 to $196 billion between 1967 and 1976, the relative decrease from 1948 to 1976 becomes almost startling. Note also that the state-level stability of proportion does not mean stagnation, but a very steady and substantial growth in actual dollars. With school costs accounting for nearly half the local government total, we can see that modern government increasingly passes by the local level, with more and more of domestic functions being handled by the state and national levels. (We say *by* the state and national levels

TABLE 2*

PERCENTAGE SHARES OF DOMESTIC DIRECT EXPENDITURES

	1902	1927	1948	1954	1962	1967	1976
Federal	17	15	23	26	27	34	33
State	10	15	26	24	24	24	25
Local	73	70	51	50	49	42	42

* Source: Frederic C. Mosher and Orville F. Poland, *The Costs of American Governments* (New York: Dodd, Mead, 1964); U.S. Bureau of the Census, *Census of Governments, 1967;* and U.S. Bureau of the Census, *Governmental Finances in 1968–69 and 1976–77.*

instead of *at* to emphasize that most of the national government's activities take place at regional and local offices around the nation. See the U.S. Government listing in your local telephone directory for confirmation that *national* does not necessarily mean *centrally* or *remotely handled.*)

The relative roles of the national and state levels may be seen in even more dramatic terms, however, if we carry this perspective one step further, subtracting from state and local levels the amount of their expenditures financed not by their own resources but out of revenue originating as grants from above. Then the shares are:

	1969	1976
Federal	43 percent	51 percent
State	29 percent	24 percent
Local	28 percent	25 percent

These figures, of activities financed by each level of government, prove conclusively that Uncle Sam is the financial senior partner of the American federal system today, quite apart from his exclusive role in external affairs.

Implications

Not unexpectedly, the constitutional and political changes that have occurred since the beginning of the century in the doctrines of American federalism have had fiscal consequences. The sharing of functions that constitutes cooperative federalism and creative federalism is seen in the cooperative financing of governmental functions. The entry of state and federal governments into operations once thought to be "merely local" is paralleled by the greater share in the financing of government operations accounted for now by these higher levels of government. Because federal grants-in-aid (the primary form of intergovernmental expenditure) have risen so rapidly in just the past few years (from $2.3 bilion in 1950 to $23.9 billion in 1970 and $91.8 billion estimated for 1982), statistics that exclude this kind of expenditure present, as we have just seen, a very incomplete and inadequate picture of the dramatically enlarged role of Washington in the financial aspects of federalism. The fiscally subordinate status of a local government is perhaps made even more sharply evident when we recall the revenue-shares picture presented earlier in this chapter: For 1968, the federal government collected 56.5 percent of all public revenues, the states 24.5 percent, and the local governments 19 percent.

In the previous chapter, Kenneth Wheare was quoted as saying that the maintenance of federalism requires that regional governments have sufficient economic resources to support themselves if they are to be truly independent and coordinate rather than subordinate to the central government. The brief examination of fiscal federalism contained in this chapter has demonstrated that the state-local governments are by no means financially independent. Furthermore, it seems beyond cavil that this financial dependence will increase over time. In fiscal 1971 more than one fifth of state-local revenues derived from federal aid. Just ten years earlier, that figure was 12 percent. If Wheare's requirements are accurate, then the fiscal facts we have just reviewed suggest that federalism in the United States is dead.

On the other hand, this position assumes what in fact needs to be questioned: Whether *financial* dependence necessarily means *programmatic* dependence. Let us now examine that assumption.

The development of the present-day pattern of fiscal federalism raises particular questions for us. We do not yet know the full implications of the pattern, and we will not know it until we have explored such questions as the following:

How does fiscal federalism relate to political federalism? Does financial contribution equal political power? If fiscal relationships do matter to federalism, which is the significant aspect—how much money is supplied by each level, or which level spends it in contact with the citizens? (The federal government is clearly dominant on the first aspect, and local governments and state-local governments together are clearly dominant with regard to the second aspect. Which matters more?) The answers to such questions cannot be determined deductively. They require examination of *how* the funds granted by a higher level to a lower level of government are given; i.e., with what strings attached, or with what purposeful insulation from control. This requires an investigation of the existing grant-in-aid system, its origins, operations, and evaluation, and of recently developed alternatives.

The next question might be: How important is the tax-expenditure linkage? That is, has the level of government that raises the money a right (or an obligation) to decide the purposes upon which it is to be spent? If one level raises the money, but allows a lower level to decide how to spend it, what are the implications for the distribution of power assumed by the concept of federalism? Although the federal government might become in time the source of more than half of state and local revenue, which would clearly make the United States a unitary rather than a federal system in its governmental finance, is it possible that this could be in fact quite consistent with continuance of a federal pattern in substantive *policy* development? In other words, could there be autonomy of state and local governments in making policy decisions regarding the purposes for which they will spend their revenues if the federal government were to turn over those funds with no strings attached? (We will focus on this question in our discussion of general revenue sharing in Chapter 4.)

We can clearly state at this point that the dominant pattern of fiscal federalism is one in which the raising of public revenue is increasingly and overwhelmingly a function of the national government; it is one in which the direct expenditures—the visible connection between the government and its suppliers, clients, and beneficiaries—are still largely in the hands of state and local governments, although with the intermediate level gradually becoming larger; and it is one in which, finally, the very rapid increase of federal financial aid to the lower levels in the past two decades has been predominantly for purposes defined by the national Congress.

The balance of state and national power and state and national policy-making authority that constitutes the essence of federalism is composed of numerous and complex elements. The instruments of change in that balance are also diverse. They include the political party system, whose decentralized pattern is often cited as both cause and effect of constitutional federalism, as well as Supreme Court decisions that impose national standards of behavior (presumably although not always actually in accord with national political majority sentiments) upon sometimes reluctant state political majorities—as most obviously in the case of civil rights. They also include the institutions and processes by which public funds are both raised and spent in pursuit of the goals of government.

We know that the overall financial picture shows great and urgent difficulty on the part of many local governments, particularly the older major cities, and relative ease on the part of the national government. Because the high inflation rate of recent years has had the unanticipated consequence of raising substantially the revenues of some state governments with at least slightly progressive income taxes as well as the revenues of the national government, the state picture is now quite mixed: Some are not in the desperate situations they were in a few years ago. On the other hand, some still are, and where state surpluses have been built up, Proposition 13-stimulated "taxpayer revolts" will probably soon erase such surpluses and perhaps create even greater difficulties than in the past by the adoption of straitjacket formulas that will reduce the flexibility of state governments.

We do not know whether further development of the pattern of rather specific grants-in-aid can contribute more to the solution of our domestic problems than can general revenue sharing and the in-between category of block grants, described and analyzed in chapter 5. Much of the remainder of this book will explore the comparative merits of these approaches to fiscal federalism. We shall also be concerned with the respective implications of these approaches for the continuance of federalism. We might have to face the possibility that what is best for the continuance of federalism is least adequate for the solving of major problems. It is to illuminate the choices that lie before us that these pages are written.

Our own position will emerge clearly in this study. We believe that the national government must exercise some leadership through leverage in order to assure that the highest standards of the citizenry as a national community are the ones in accord with which nationally raised revenues are expended. Nevertheless, we have come to view efforts growing out of the New Federalism concept more favorably as we study the experience and data of recent years. Regardless of personal views, we have made every effort to present a balanced and objective description and analysis of the factors involved and the choices that face us all.

3

Grants-in-Aid: The Cutting Edge of Intergovernmental Relations

The best proof that the states'-rights model of federalism (as a system of government in which the central and regional levels each operate in their own exclusive sphere) is dead lies in the grant-in-aid system, which uses a fiscal relationship as a basis for policy making and programmatic cooperation. This system constitutes the complete embodiment of Grodzins's conception of federalism—although it remains to be seen whether the Grodzins corollary of decentralized policy making is also validated, since the sharing of functions does not necessarily mean the absence of a dominant policy-making role by one of the partners. As we describe major features of the grant-in-aid system, let's keep in mind as an overall orienting question the degree to which federal fiscal sharing in programs operated directly by state and local governments produces federal influence or power. It will quickly become clear that the answer does not lie in the sphere of quick and easy generalization; rather, it is in the area of "it depends"—on the type of grant, on the type of substantive program, on the interest group and political configurations surrounding each program, and so forth. It is probably safe to agree, however, with William H. Young's assertion that "the most powerful engine in this century for reshaping national-state relations has been the 'grant-in-aid' system of national financing of state and local activities."[1]

Grants-in-aid may be defined as money payments furnished by a higher to a lower level of government to be used for specified purposes and subject to conditions spelled out in law or administrative regulation. Grants are thus distinguished from, although first cousins to, the concept of general revenue sharing, which means money given by one level of government to another *without* advance specification of purpose and *without* specified conditions. The range of functions in which federal-state-local cooperation takes place by means of grant-in-aid includes cooperative state agricultural experiment stations (the granddaddy of the system, started in 1887), vocational education, aid to the blind and to families with dependent children, airport construction, urban renewal, water treatment works construction, defense-related educational activities, mass transportation, air pollution control, highway beautification, waste disposal facilities, school libraries, adult work training, and even educational television. Health, highways, welfare, and employment training are the major categories of aided functions, with Medicaid the largest at $12.4 billion in 1980. The precise number of grant programs currently in operation depends a bit upon one's definition. Using the criterion of separate authorizations, the Advisory Commission on Intergovernmental Relations (ACIR) estimated a total of 492 categorical grant-in-aid programs in 1978, plus five block grants programs.

This astonishing number of grant-in-aid programs is more than matched by the exploding rate of increase in the dollar volume of appropriations accounted for by the grants. The 1980 estimate was $82.9 billion, compared with an actual

1970 figure of $24 billion and a 1961 figure of a mere $7
billion. In fiscal 1947, right after the Second World War,
grants-in-aid amounted to only $1.668 billion. Making all due
allowance for the impact of inflation upon these actual dollar
figures, it is clear that Congress is very fond of the grant-in-
aid idea. This is, as we have seen, partly in response to the
state-local fiscal crisis and the consequent need for revenue;
but it is also (and perhaps in larger part) a response to
pressures from federal agencies, functional specialists in and
out of government, and specific interest groups, all of whom
have become well aware of the potentials of the strategy
under which one obtains action in all states by using the
leverage one has at a single pressure point—that is, the
national Congress.

The historical origins of the grant-in-aid system actually
antedate the Constitution. The Land Ordinance of 1785 provided that lot number 16 of each township carved out of
federal lands should be reserved for maintenance of public
schools. Although most of the early grants were in the form
of land rather than cash, there were a few of the latter kind.
In 1808, there was a congressional appropriation of $200,000
to assist the development of state militia; and the early 1800s
also saw cash aid for railroads and canals, supplementing the
very large land grants given to the railroads. By 1915, the
dollar volume of cash grants had only reached $5 million.
The major categories were agricultural extension, highways,
and, after 1917, vocational education. From World War I
until the New Deal, these programs amounted to about $100
million annually. During the New Deal there was a spurt in
grant programs with the new federal aid being associated
with Social Security programs of public assistance and unemployment agencies, aid for state and local planning, and,
in 1937, the first public housing program, under which the
federal government provided long-term loans for state and

local housing authorities to construct low-rent housing and grants for slum clearance.[2]

The programs of the 1930s were the first to require substantial federal supervision and the first to impose management conditions upon the grants. Perhaps the most notable conditions were those for financial audits and, under the Social Security system, provision that state and local personnel participating be selected and administered under a merit system. Most of the programs in the early years had fairly stiff matching requirements: The receiving unit of government had to put up a dollar of its own money for each dollar it received in the form of a federal grant. In the 1960s, however, the great majority of programs were enacted with much more than 50-percent federal participation, often 100 percent under project grants whose major purpose was to stimulate innovation. As of 1978, about 150 of the grant programs provided 100-percent national financing, and another 200 had low matching requirements.

Grants-in-aid constitute a major social invention of our time and are the prototypical, although not the statistically dominant (they now constitute over 20 percent of domestic federal outlays) form of federal domestic involvement. Although grants serve many different purposes and have various political and economic rationales, we suspect that the most important single reason for their popularity among both politicians and professionals of the functional areas aided is that the grant device bypasses all the difficult questions of governmental structure in a federal division of authority. In this respect, grants constitute a halfway house very similar to the post-Keynesian system of economic stabilization and business regulation in which the public sector has a decisive influence upon private economic activity but exerts it through indirect means that avoid the structural question of capitalism versus socialism. By using grants, one doesn't have to face the question: At which level of government does this function belong? If the activity is traditionally a local one, its direct operation can remain there while its financial problems are solved with federal aid. If the federal government wants to inject its sense of values and priorities into the shaping of a program, the categorical grant provides a vehicle for programmatic leverage without necessitating removal of the whole function from local hands.

Types of Grants

There are several different ways to characterize the subdivisions of the grant-in-aid system. One important division is between *categorical* and *block* grants. While there is—as always with such analytic distinctions—a gray area of overlap, categorical grants are by and large intended for specifically and narrowly defined purposes, leaving very little discretionary room on the part of a recipient government. Block grants (see chapter 5) are broader in scope, and although tied to a clearly stated area (such as health, social services, or community development), they do not specify the exact subjects of permitted expenditure and hence create much larger zones of discretion on the part of the receiving government or agency. ACIR defines a block grant as one that "goes chiefly to general purpose governmental units in accordance with a statutory formula for use in a variety of activities within a broad functional area largely at the recipient's discretion." Categorical grants have a much greater potential impact on federalism—changing the locus of policy making more sharply from the state-local to the national level—than do block grants. In terms of federalism, state-local discretion in the use of federally provided funds is the functional equivalent of fiscal autonomy.

As part of his New Federalism, it was President Nixon's

intent to create several areas of *special revenue sharing* (SRS) which would have been like general revenue sharing in the absence of strings, procedural or substantive, but like block grants in being designated for a specific (though broad) area of activity. Law enforcement, transportation, community development, education, and manpower training were among the areas for which SRS plans were proposed. None were enacted as such, but two major block grants, CETA and CDGB (explained in chapter 5), did emerge partly in response to the SRS proposals.

A second basis for distinguishing among grants is found in the criteria for distribution. *Formula* grants are to be distinguished from *project* grants by this means. As the name implies, the formula grant is one whose funds are divided among all eligible recipients on the basis of some announced criterion that is applied proportionately across the board and without any discretion in the hands of the grant-giving officials. An example is public assistance grants for aid to the blind. Under this program, the national government promises to match state payments of benefits to blind persons in accordance with a statutory ratio. The needy blind in every state are eligible, and the national government is committed to supplying its share of the benefits for as many persons as the state welfare departments certify as eligible. Formula grants are distributed to all eligible jurisdictions as a matter of "right." The discretion, if there is any, lies in the hands of the recipient governments that decide how much matching money they want to use to obtain a particular federal grant. Federal influence under formula grants lies in the administrative requirements that accompany the grant rather than in the substance of the grant.

In project grants, which require specific approval by federal agency officials of the proposal made by a government or agency, the likelihood of federal influence and control is decidedly greater. Project grants are made to meet specific problems and are not spread among all potential recipients according to any fixed proportions. Although every community in the country may be eligible for a waste treatment plant grant, for example, the funds available for the program will sharply limit the number of communities that can be aided. In such a situation, the community whose proposal most nearly satisfies the definitions of appropriate action in the minds of the federal officials administering the grant program will be the successful one. As President Nixon said in one of his revenue-sharing messages, "Because competition between localities for limited Federal dollars is most intense, local officials are highly motivated to meet both the formal requirements and the informal preferences of Federal officials as they file their applications."

With about 322 of the 492 grant-in-aid programs being of the project type, there is considerable room for state-local discretion in "shopping around" to decide which grants to apply for. Indeed, because proposal preparation requires both energy and administrative sophistication, it may be that the project grant often does not go where the financial need is greatest. As of 1975, 31 percent of categorical grant funds were in project grant form.

Both the advantages and the problems of project grants are well illustrated by an anecdote from the history of the community mental health centers. A *New York Times* story of June 29, 1970, noted that "it is federal policy to promote local initiatives." (That's an interesting paradox in itself—that local initiatives now require a national government stimulus!) The particular initiative referred to was the development of community mental health centers under a program inaugurated by the National Institute of Mental Health. This federal grant program was too successful: It encouraged the creation of more mental health centers than the federal government said it could afford to support, even though they had all been begun in anticipation of federal aid for staffing. In fiscal 1970, some 123 new grant requests were made and approved by the Institute, but the agency then found that it could fund only 63 of these projects. As of a year later, 27 of the carry-over applications had been funded. With new applications coming in, the fiscal year ending June 30, 1971, saw 55 staffing grant applications recommended for approval but left stranded without funds. Perhaps 20 of these found other sources of support and so became operational for some services.[3]

Purposes of Grants

Decisions regarding when to use formula grants and when to use project grants, and evaluation of the merits of each type, depend partly on the purposes for which one has a grant at all. We sometimes assume that the purpose of all federal grants-in-aid is financial in nature: to supplement inadequate state-local resources. This is too simple. At least as important as the purely financial objective are the following:

1. *To establish minimum national standards in some program that exists in all states, but at widely differing levels.* Examples would include air and water pollution control programs that set parts-per-million standards regarding allowable levels of pollutants, and pesticide controls (as with DCPB), which grower pressures might well emasculate in some states in the absence of a federally mandated minimum standard.

2. *Equalization of resources.* This objective is closely related to the first one. The emphasis here is upon the use of the federal tax system to apply the Robin Hood principle: to take more money from the states with higher per capita

incomes and transfer it to those with lower per capita incomes, enabling the latter to upgrade their public services. Many federal formula grant programs have had sliding scales that vary federal contributions from one third to two thirds, inversely related to the capacity of receiving states to raise their own funds. The trend, however, is away from equalization.

3. *To improve the substantive adequacy of state programs*. Under project programs particularly, in the process of inviting, aiding in the design of, reviewing, and approving proposals from state-local agencies, officials of the grant-giving agency have an opportunity to provide technical assistance in acordance with the highest professional standards. Inasmuch as only a few states are able to compete with the national government in attracting outstanding professional talent, such technical assistance can be an important vehicle for upgrading the quality of public services at the state level. Graves evaluated the standard-setting impact of the Hill-Burton Program for planning and constructing hospitals with federal aid with these summary comments:

> The introduction of a continuing state-wide planning program is a landmark in the field of hospital and medical facility planning and construction, while the utilization of standards of adequacy and the development of patterns for distributing facilities within a State has resulted in important gains in hospital planning and better distribution of health facilities. Another important accomplishment of the program has been the development for the first time of minimum standards of design, construction and equipment for hospitals and other types of medical health facilities.[4]

4. *Concentration of research resources*. A related way in which the federal government may improve state programs, concentrate a "critical mass" of attention in a given area,

and avoid useless state duplication and the frittering away of energies in many efforts is exemplified in air pollution research grants from the Environmental Protection Administration. If California, New York, Idaho, and other states with air pollution problems were to go their independent ways on their research, there would be a great deal of money wasted, and no state alone could afford to spend enough to do an adequate job. Federal grants can be the catalyst for bringing a unified research program into being out of the cooperative efforts of all interested states.

5. *The stimulation of experimentation and the demonstration of new approaches* are major objectives of a high proportion of the project grant programs in the areas of health care, education, human resources development, and community development. Sometimes the stimulus is not for a innovative program but simply to get more communities to do something quite ordinary that they don't get around to on their own. The sewage treatment plant program inaugurated in the late 1950s is a good example. The number of treatment plants under construction jumped several-fold in the first three years of operation of this grant program. Apparently federal money stimulated the cupidity of local governments, if nothing else, making it hard for them not to do something for which the federal government would pay half the cost.

Perhaps the most experimental and stimulative—too much so for many politicians involved—of all federal grant programs were the community action programs under the Office of Economic Opportunity in the late sixties. OEO grants encouraged substantive experimentation in treating the symptoms and causes of poverty in more free-wheeling ways than the traditional social welfare agency pattern had permitted. Class action law suits on behalf of the victims of finance companies and installment merchandisers also sufficiently proved their worth so that President Nixon initiated separate institutionalization for this concept.

Even more stimulative of experiment than the substantive programs undertaken by OEO was the unheard-of process of encouraging the poor to participate in the design and implementation of their own programs. OEO grants also encouraged recipients to organize to work their way into American politics, or, as the late E. E. Schattschneider put it, to work their way into the pressure system from which they had traditionally been excluded.[5] It is safe to say in the case of OEO grants that the experimentation in clientele policy making generated by the innocuous-sounding phrase *maximum feasible participation* ended up being a good deal more experimental than nine tenths of the government officials and legislators associated with the program ever expected—or wanted. The perhaps quixotic ideal of "participatory democracy" has been at least partly realized in actual practice: Through the operation of grants to community action programs, participatory democracy is more than a theory.

Let us note here an interesting point about the thesis of federalism as a system that encourages the use of the constituent units as laboratories, with an opportunity for successful results to be applied through the national level of federalism to other constituent units. The induced changes in political structure and in substantive policies that made OEO grants so controversial did not take place according to the mythological formula. Instead of a few states or localities trying out an idea that had welled up spontaneously at the local level, these astonishing experiments came about because an agency of the central government (drawing upon some expertise developed in a foundation-sponsored program for dealing with youth problems) *mandated* a new kind and degree of local citizen participation as a condition for receiving national government funds. Alliances developed between functional professionals working in the local Community Action Programs (CAPs) and in OEO headquarters—alliances that constituted a kind of functional federalism as a conscious alternative to the predominantly status quo orientation of the regular government structures under the control of local elites. In short, the OEO grant program conclusively proved that experimentation *can* be directed from above. Indeed, sometimes that is the only way it can be started at the local level. Two very significant examples of social experimentation that were directly developed by the federal government, and probably could not have come about otherwise, are the Housing Allowance and Negative Income programs. These are important both as examples of national leadership in programmatic innovation and as constituting perhaps the largest-scale social science equivalents to physical science R&D (research and development) that America has ever seen.

6. *Improvement of state-local administrative structure and operation.* Since the adoption of the public assistance grant programs in the mid-thirties and the 1939 amendment to the Social Security Act that established a merit system requirement for participating state agencies, the general administrative requirements attached to a great number of federal grants have induced grant-receiving governments to professionalize their organizational structures and their personnel and financial practices. Merit system and auditing requirements have had double effects. Directly, they have established new standards of competence and accountability in the agencies handling federal funds. Indirectly, these standards have constituted, if only by contrast, benchmarks against which to measure the quality of operation of state agencies not subject to federal supervision. While a few states have always been the equal (even occasionally the superior) of the national government with regard to administrative quality, the great majority have been extremely laggard in adopting modern management knowledge. The

national government has therefore played an indispensable role in relaying to the states the management knowledge it has itself developed and assimilated from the most advanced private business practice. From the standpoint of maintaining a healthy federalism, the administrative improvement impact of the federal grant system upon the states may have been at least as important (by improving state-local government effectiveness) as the provision of funds.

7. *Encouragement of general social objectives.* The "boilerplate" provisions of federal programs (those provisions that are automatically included in every grant agreement between the grantor agency and the grantee government) have also been used as inducements to attain unrelated social objectives. The most notable among these is, of course, the nondiscrimination clause that has made grants-in-aid a potent lever in the struggle to persuade the more recalcitrant state governments to provide public services equitably to their minority populations.

8. *Minimize the apparent federal role.* Perhaps the most important political achievement of the grant system is to have solved the apparent dilemma arising from the American electorate's contradictory desires (a) to attack problems that the state and local governments lacked the resources to handle while (b) not enlarging the federal government. The solution to the dilemma is that the federal role is in fact enlarged, always in financial terms and often in programmatic terms, without that enlargement being apparent either in the size of the federal civil service or in the number of occasions upon which the individual citizen deals with a national functionary. It is a nice way of having one's cake while eating it. Recent Presidents of the United States have prided themselves on reducing the size of the federal bureaucracy, or at least in reducing its rate of growth to very minimal proportions. They have also prided themselves on

the increasing help they have given to the solution of domestic problems through new and enlarged grant programs. They have never, however, put the two together so as to acknowledge that the first claim could be made only because a result of the second claim was to increase greatly the size of the bureaucracy at the state-local levels (as mentioned earlier). Of course, we shouldn't push this too far. It is certainly still true that direct federal operation of the funds and programs represented by the $80 billion plus of current federal grants-in-aid would considerably increase the federal "presence."

Rationalizing the Grant System

Closely related to yet conceptually distinguishable from the functions served by a particular grant program are the economic and political rationales underlying the entire grant system. If one sees grants-in-aid as occurring largely in areas once thought to be the more or less exclusive provinces of state-local governments under a federalized "division of labor," then the question becomes: What justification is there for the national government to enter the picture, even through grants-in-aid, let alone through direct action programs? From an economic standpoint, there are two parts to the answer. First, the simple fact elaborated earlier, that it is much easier to raise the needed revenue for public service operations at the national level than at the local level, although the problems for which the revenue is needed still have to be handled at the local level. Second, there stands the doctrine of external or "spillover" benefits. This says that when an expenditure produces benefits that are felt beyond (i.e., spill over) the jurisdiction of the governmental unit making the expenditure, it is proper that all benefiting jurisdictions share in the cost. Otherwise, some of them are engaged in freeloading.[6]

Education provides a handy example. It provides tangible financial benefits both to the individuals educated and to the taxing jurisdictions in which they reside. The reason for this is simple: The more education a person has, on the average, the greater will be his/her earnings, and the greater the earnings, the larger the amount of taxes he/she will pay. Less tangibly, but perhaps more important in the long run, an educated populace is an essential precondition to effective democracy. If, then, the per pupil expenditure on education in California or New York is much higher than the national average of the states, every time a person educated in one of those two states moves to a state with a smaller per capita education expenditure, the latter state receives external benefits that it has not paid for. In a nation with the mobility rate that ours has (20 percent of the population moves each year), and given the fact that school system expenditures vary as much between communities in any one state as they do among states (because of heavy reliance upon property taxes whose yield varies greatly from one location to another), the external benefits attributable to public education expenditures extend to the entire nation. At another level, that of graduate education in the universities, the spillover aspect is even more notable. A National Science Board report recommending increased federal aid says:

Graduate institutions are national resources. The graduate student body, especially at larger institutions and at the doctoral level, is drawn from a wide geographic area, frequently from the entire Nation, while trained scientists and engineers provided by graduate education are also highly mobile and distribute themselves nationally as career opportunities warrant.

. . . The maintenance of an adequate supply of well-prepared teachers of science and engineering for service at all educational levels is a matter of national concern.[7]

According to a leading authority on intergovernmental fiscal relations, George F. Break, categorical grants-in-aid are economically justifiable only on the basis of and to the extent of their externalities or spillover benefits. He suggests that in evaluating grant-in-aid programs, we ask of each program whether it generates external benefits, the exact nature of those benefits, and how important they are. By rating the importance of the projected benefits, and assuming that we can measure in some way the extent of the benefits, we have a basis for determining the appropriate federal share of expenditure in that area. The conceptualization here is somewhat in advance of our empirical knowledge (while we know what to measure, we do not yet know how to measure it in many instances), but the reasoning is generally persuasive. Writing in the summer, and in a state that receives a very substantial influx of summer visitors, we can well see a spillover benefit from the recreational resources provided by the state of California, and therefore a good reason for national taxes to help support those resources, since many non-Californians will be enjoying them.

Even in the absence of spillover benefits, there is a strong political rationale for federal grants. One of the more thoughtful analyses has been provided by political scientist Phillip Monypenny. In a 1960 article he argued that federal grant programs were a response to a

> coalition which resorts to a mixed federal-state program because it is not strong enough in individual states to secure its program, and because it is not united enough to be able to achieve a wholly federal program against the opposition which a specific program would engender.[8]

It is a truism of the politics of policy making in the United States that some interest groups are more effective at state and local levels and others at the national level. Labor unions, for example, have their membership concentrated in about one third of the states. Since these are the large industrial states with many congressmen and many electoral votes for the Presidency, their weight is considerable at the national capital. At the state level, it may be considerable in ten or fifteen states, but falls off to zero or perhaps even a negative impact in many other states. Many industrial interest groups, on the other hand, find that they receive more sympathetic hearings at state capitals than in Washington. Any group that wants something done at the state level, but has its greatest political clout at the national level, will naturally turn toward a grant-in-aid approach in order to combine the two. We will see in chapter 4 that general revenue sharing complicates this.

Further, an important impetus toward grant-in-aid programs arises from the most fundamental feature of American federalism—that to achieve action at the state level means to mount a campaign in 50 different locations, while to mount one at the national level requires and encourages centralized, unified action in a single place, a task that is generally easier to achieve. Once the national government has been persuaded to enact a program, the leverage of "free money" will encourage many of the states to join in. Granting that ancillary political campaigns will sometimes be needed at the state level, the effort becomes a good deal more effective when preceded by national authorizing legislation. The reasons, incidentally, for not seeking a directly national program are not only the lack of sufficient political power to achieve that possible goal, but also the fact that wholly national action runs into more ideological obstacles than does federal aid. Also one simply may have no desire to substitute national for state action, but only wish to beef up state action.

A final reason for bringing the federal government into previously state-local problem solving through the grant-in-aid device is that the definition of what is national and what is local has changed, as well as our conception of federalism, which has gone from a competitive to a cooperative image. In terms of *Realpolitik* it has been well said that "any objective is manifestly and significantly national in character which survives the arduous, lengthy 'testing process' that Congress provides with its polycentric power structure and limited majority norms."[9] That may sound too simple or even too cynical, yet when one tries to grapple with the question of what is a national problem, or what situations warrant national action, it is difficult to find any other single criterion that will fit every instance. Only two generalizations seem to be quite certain. One is that many more problems today than in the past are national in the sense of being affected by developments elsewhere in the nation or having their own impact upon other parts of the nation. Our society has become thoroughly interdependent in its economy, its transportation and communication patterns, etc. Second, what can safely be left to local discretion is not answerable across the board; it depends on particular functions. This is true not only of relations between the national and state governments but even of relationships between a city as a whole and its neighborhoods. Consider, for example, James L. Sundquist's comment in a discussion of the implications of decentralization under the Model Cities program:

The extent to which the city can defer to neighborhood opinion varies by function. It may be able to accept neighborhood control on local rezoning issues, for example, while to defer to it at all on the enforcement of an open housing ordinance would be to nullify the law. Each neighborhood cannot have its own freeway plan. Each cannot be the hospital center of the community. Salaries paid to employees of neighborhood organizations need to be standardized in the interests of equity. Equality of public services among neighborhoods has to be equalized.[10]

Moreover, there seems to be hardly anything that we think of as local that does not have national aspects: Even the very local function of police protection today has national dimensions in the training of local police officers at the FBI academy and in the research and development aimed at crime prevention through grants under the Omnibus Crime Control and Safe Streets Act of 1968.

One of the major official efforts to lay down the conditions justifying national government action concerning domestic problems was that of the Commission on Intergovernmental Relations. Its report to President Eisenhower in 1955 specified the following conditions:

1. When only the national government has the resources for the job—e.g., defense, economic stabilization;
2. When the activity cannot be handled within the geographic-jurisdictional limits of the lesser governments —e.g., radio and television frequency allocations and regulation;
3. When national uniformity is required—e.g., the provision of currency (how broad a category might that be today);
4. When one state's action or inaction may hurt other states—e.g., hindrances to interstate commerce or resource conservation;
5. When a state fails to protect basic political and civil rights that apply throughout the United States.[11]

Although we characterize the commission's efforts as "major," these criteria are really useless, for they beg the difficult questions: How does one decide which activities "cannot be handled" at the lower level? How does one decide when national uniformity is required? The answer, of course, lies in empirical case-by-case examination of each problem. When such examination reveals that the problem cannot be resolved effectively at the local level, then one has a national problem.

Unemployment, for example, is clearly a national problem: There is nothing that any one city or state can do to solve a problem of cyclical unemployment in an interdependent national economy. Let's take a harder case: how about air pollution? In one sense, it is clearly local. That is to say, it could largely be solved in the Los Angeles area irrespective of what is or is not done about solving it in New York. At the same time, there are dimensions that go far beyond Los Angeles. One is the need for national action to assure that automobile manufacturers in Detroit turn out the least smog-producing cars posible. Another is that the elimination of smog requires a great deal more scientific research than Los Angeles alone could afford to provide; and this is equally true of research related to solar energy or nuclear power. Since the research that will aid Los Angeles in solving its smog problems would also help with the air pollution problems of Idaho and New York and Chicago and New Orleans, and since it would be pointless for each of those jurisdictions to duplicate the research performed by the others, it makes a great deal of sense for the national government to participate in the financing of that research.

Some problems are national in that they are indivisible across the nation. Unemployment, as mentioned, is one of these. Other problems are national despite divisibility because they exist in cities throughout the country. Child abuse and battered spouses are unfortunate notable examples. Although their manifestations are localized to given places and times, their roots appear to lie deep in the structure of our society, in aspects of our culture that are national rather than locally differentiable. Just to complicate the picture a little bit more, consider President Eisenhower's intervention in the Little Rock school integration crisis in 1957. Federal troops were called into play when one high school failed to comply with constitutional requirements announced by the Supreme Court. Although national action was taken, it was very much pinpointed to a specific local situation. Therefore it exemplifies the proposition that the national government *can* take local circumstances into account in its actions, perhaps just as well as can a local agency.

In an important book on the problems of administering grant-in-aid programs, James L. Sundquist argues that about 1960 the grant-in-aid system underwent a fundamental change. Prior to that date, he writes, "the typical federal assistance program did not involve an expressly stated *national* purpose. It was instituted, rather, as a means of helping state or local governments accomplish *their* objectives." Legislation passed since 1960 is characterized by "forthright declarations of national purpose, experimental and flexible approaches to the achievement of those purposes, and close federal supervision and control to ensure that the national purposes are served."[12] He suggests that aid for highways, hospitals, sewage treatment plants, and the building of airports all constitute instances in which the federal grants really are *in aid* of state-local functions. On the other hand, in the cases of urban renewal, area redevelopment, manpower development, the poverty program, and compensatory education, he contends that the grants are for the purpose of getting the state and local governments to participate in the administration of programs designed to achieve objectives initially chosen by the national government. Incidentally, he includes urban renewal, dating from 1949, in the latter group as an early exception.

Whether the original impetus for a grant program in a particular area came from state-local officials, federal officials, or national legislators may be important in terms of legislative history, but does not matter much in the operation of programs once enacted. Even if the states originally set the goal of "getting the farmers out of the mud," when the federal government enters the highway picture by supplementing state financing, isn't it making that goal a national goal also? Since the federal government does not aid every single state and local purpose, in the process of selecting those purposes that it will aid it is making a determination of the state-local functions in which there is the greatest national interest. As Sundquist himself later suggests, public attitudes pass through different phases as major domestic problems develop. First, a problem is seen as local. Second, federal aid is proposed to help the states solve *their* problem. Finally, the problem is redefined as being national and requiring a national solution which the states merely help to bring about.

So we come back to the beginning. Those things are national and justify grant programs which the Congress *says* are national. The concepts of local and national interest are amorphous at best. What matters for present purposes is that both constitutionally and politically, we have as a nation accepted the notion that it is appropriate for the national community to embed its scale of values (i.e., those values that a majority of national legislators can agree upon) in programs that offer state and local governments financial inducements to be persuaded that the national scale of values should also be the local priorities. In assessing the long-range trend line of federalism, this is to say that the balance is shifting toward the dominance of national majorities over state and local majorities, with cooperative action toward national objectives replacing the futile deadlock of the old competitive dual federalism.

The System's Accomplishments

Although complete evaluation of the grant-in-aid system we have been describing must await further analysis and elucidation of revenue sharing and block grants as widely heralded alternatives, it is possible and desirable to draw up a preliminary balance sheet of the system's accomplishments and problems. The most obvious accomplishment of federal grants is to enable state and local governments to do much more for their citizens than they could afford to do with their own resources. To say that grant-in-aid funds equal one-third of state-local revenues from their own sources is to say that those governments would do one-third less for their citizens without federal aid.

If, as the late Morton Grodzins and his disciples have argued, modern federalism is and must be cooperative rather than competitive, then one has to say that the grant-in-aid device constitutes a major social invention. It is what makes cooperative federalism a functioning reality instead of just a constitutional lawyer's phase. Intergovernmental cooperation also does exist in forms other than grants-in-aid. (An example would be local, state, and national police forces sharing information and techniques.) But the grant relationship is far and away the most decisive means of intergovernmental cooperation today. Because it solves or at least ameliorates the fiscal problem of modern federalism while permitting widely varying degrees of federal influence along with the funds, it makes the continuation of formal federalism possible.

An advantage of the grant system that is not always given sufficient attention is the way in which it enables the national government to provide technical assistance to state and local governments. Since, by and large, the national government can better tap top-drawer professional talent, whether of highway engineering, social insurance, housing-market analysis, or education, than can a multitude of state and local governmental bodies, it is in a position to bring such talent to bear on local problems in a way that the jurisdiction having the problem could never afford to do autonomously. Further, even when the professional innovation takes place initially in an individual state, the existence of a national grant-in-aid program provides a means for information transfer from the initiating state to all others. If the federal grant system had never been started, state-local government would often be acting at a much lower level of professional quality than is now the case when the federal government sets the standards.

We mentioned earlier that there is a varying structure of interest-group power at different levels of government. Because of this, the grant-in-aid system also permits the national government to respond to societal needs not politically strong in many states, stimulating states to act in areas that would otherwise be neglected because of the short-sighted, status quo views of local elites. The poverty program, aid to education, community mental health, and environmental protection are all areas that fit this description in a number of states. The grant-in-aid system accomplishes an in-between answer to what would otherwise be a stalemate: The state-local level can't or won't solve all its problems with its own resources, yet the electorate appears not to want the entire responsibility transferred to the national level. Therefore, through grants-in-aid we find a way to put the resources where the problems are: to get the jobs done. It also seems probable that the total public sector expenditure on domestic problems is augmented beyond what it would otherwise be. That is, it is politically easier to spend the money through a grant program than it would be either to spend it on a directly national program or to get equivalent amounts appropriated by the totality of the state legislatures.

Finally, there is a somewhat tangible accomplishment of the grant-in-aid system that may be more important than the financial resources the system provides. This accomplishment consists of injecting more of a public interest perspective into the operations of state-local governments than would be likely without the stimulus. Walter Lippman once defined the public interest as "what men would choose if they saw clearly, thought rationally, acted disinterestedly and benevolently."[13] The national government comes much closer to filling that prescription than can the state and local governments, particularly as regards fullness of resources. With a private individual or a family, if one has barely enough money to buy food and clothing for today, one is likely to let the future take care of itself. So it is with governments: What is needed tomorrow will often be sacrificed to what makes things easier today. Similarly, what will be of general benefit to everyone, but perhaps not always of specific benefit to any group, tends to get pushed aside. The development of recreation areas for a growing population exemplifies both of these tendencies and problems. As George Break writes,

> There is a strong possibility that states, with their continuous preoccupation with short-run financing problems, will under-value, or even ignore, the future benefits to an ever-growing population of a widespread system of public parks and wilderness areas. From its position of greater fiscal affluence, the federal government is in a better position to judge these matters and to finance the necessary land acquisitions before it is too late.[14]

One can hardly blame the retiree on a fixed Social Security pension who takes a short-sighted view and votes against community needs in order to hold down the property tax that constitutes his primary financial burden. The federal grant-in-aid system is an essential and effective device for counteracting the short-run tendency, and it thereby encourages state and local governments to improve the quality of living for the future.

The System's Problems

Like every other human invention, the grant-in-aid system lacks perfection. Four types of problems that the system either fails to solve or self-creates need to be mentioned. First, the strong trend toward project grants, which are very useful for targeting the aid and for stimulating innovation, also has less desirable consequences. Project grants tend to run counter to the need for equalization of resources among jurisdictions. Those state and local governments which have the best professional staffs are likely to prepare the best proposals and thus receive the most project aid. Yet they are likely also to be the jurisdictions that are already most alert and have the best financial bases, and therefore the least need. There is perhaps an exception to this in the case of the very largest cities, which have both high degrees of professionalism and some very poverty-stricken neighborhoods. But for many other communities, there is a real question whether the project grant system may simply make the rich richer, as it were. Closely related is the fact that the awarding of funds on the basis of competitive proposals places a premium on "grantsmanship," a rapidly developing form of what is more generally known as "gamesmanship." As noted earlier, relative capability in manipulating language to please federal administrators may become more important than relative objective need in determining which communities receive the most aid.

A related set of charges sometimes made against the entire grant-in-aid system (rather than just specifically against project grants) is that it tends to skew state-local budgets.

The argument is that, to the extent that grants require matching funds from the receiving government, state legislatures and city councils will be coerced into putting their money where the grants are, even if the areas are not those of greatest local need. It is hard to resist a program that enables one dollar to become two or three when the same dollar has no "multiplier" effect of this kind when used for some other area. Since grants are fairly tightly defined and do not cover all possible areas of state-local need, their inflexibility perhaps requires that receiving governments be overly flexible in accommodating to Washington's priorities.

This problem may be somewhat lessened today, as compared with 15 years ago, because of the proliferation of grant authorizations. There are now so many grant programs for so many different purposes that, although each is very narrow, the local government can get what it wants by picking and choosing among the programs it decides to enter.

The other side of the coin is that the proliferation of programs has created a very substantial coordination problem at both the giving and receiving levels of the grant system. As the Advisory Commission on Intergovernmental Relations has said,

> Excessive categorization and overlapping of grants create administrative problems at all levels and handicap the development of a coordinated attack on community problems. . . . State and local governments may be bewildered as to the differences between seemingly like programs or uncertain as to whether they are using the more appropriate program; . . . Confusion is aggravated by the existence of varying requirements under similar programs, which may cause applicants to seek the program which seems most attractive from the standpoint, say, of non-Federal matching required although overall considerations, such as the specific uses as to which the money can be put, may make it less attractive.[15]

79

When communities are whole entities, but programs for their development are separately categorized and separately administered by separate agencies, some classic confusions result. One such instance concerned conflict regarding an urban renewal development that had been approved by one agency for a location through which another planned a freeway.

Finally, the grant-in-aid system can, of course, do nothing to help the states and cities directly as regards their lack of funds for services that lie outside the aided categories. Moreover, to the extent that aid programs call for matching grants, the city or state may be simply more hard-pressed to finance its unaided services.

Primarily because of these last two problems associated with the existing grant-in-aid system—the proliferation of narrowly specific categories and the inability of the grant system to solve the problem of inadequate financing for unaided services (such as fire departments)—and as a matter of great ideological concern over the "federal octopus" in some quarters—a great deal of enthusiasm has recently been expressed by both liberals and conservatives for various plans by which categorical grants would be supplemented by the devices of the New Federalism. In the next chapter, we turn to a description and evaluation of revenue sharing as it has been conceptualized and experienced since 1972.

4

Revenue Sharing: A Case of Arrested Development

On October 20, 1972, President Nixon signed the State and Local Fiscal Assistance Act, more commonly known as general revenue sharing (GRS).[1] Characterized by Nixon as a "new American Revolution" by which power and authority would be turned back to the people, GRS has been called a milestone in fiscal federalism by its enthusiastic supporters.

The concept of revenue sharing is quite simple. Since 1972 the federal government, through the Office of Revenue Sharing in the Treasury Department, has been mailing checks to over 39,000 general-purpose governments, Alaskan villages, Indian tribes, and the 50 state capitals with the allocations based on an automatic transfer formula. From 1972 through 1976, $6.65 billion annually was transferred from the federal treasury to eligible subnational governments, and 1976 amendments extended GRS for three and three-quarter years and authorized another $25.6 billion through 1980.

While the total dollar amount is hardly significant (the federal government transferred over $50 billion in fiscal 1979 to state and local governments through other programs), the concept behind GRS is quite different from that of earlier federal aid programs. GRS is based on transferring federal revenue to subnational governments with as few federal guidelines (strings) as possible. By restricting federal involvement in the decision-making process at the subnational level, state and local elected officials can decide on their *own* priorities, goals, and funding levels for specific programs. This is quite a departure from the conditional categorical grant programs of the 1960s and has been rightfully dubbed a "New Federalism." It is a new model in that it is a hybrid of cooperative federalism—the federal government fiscally assisting subnational governments to achieve their own objectives—and dual federalism—the ideological jargon of states' rights and local control.

While the long-run implications of the New Federalism may very well be to increase the fiscal dependency of state and local governments, the short run (or short-sighted) implications are conceptualized as applications of older models of fiscal federalism in which the autonomy of each level is stressed.

Historical Background

Few policy initiatives have had as interesting a lineage as revenue sharing. In 1958, then-Representative Melvin Laird (R. Wisc.) introduced a revenue-sharing bill in the House of Representatives. It received no attention. In 1960, Professor Walter W. Heller, a liberal Democrat and economist at the University of Minnesota, proposed a specific version of revenue sharing which was later to become known as the "Heller plan." It did not receive any more attention than Laird's bill had. From January 1961 until June 1964, Heller was chairman of the Council of Economic Advisers in the Kennedy-Johnson administrations, where he was able to proselytize quietly for the revenue-sharing concept. Not until almost the end of his tenure, however, was serious work done on the concept in the executive branch. When federal personal income taxes were reduced in 1964, some of the advocates of the "new economics" believed that federal budgetary surpluses would result anyway, and that these surpluses would create a drag on economic activity. As political liberals, most of these economists feared that the existence of surpluses would inevitably produce demands for further tax cuts, despite what they considered to be a great need to spend the additional funds in the public sector rather than return them to individual taxpayers' pockets. Apparently they felt that there would be inadequate political muscle to ensure that the prospective surpluses were turned into federal expenditures through expansion of existing domestic general welfare programs. Revenue sharing—the Heller plan—therefore seemed an attractive alternative, one that would bring more funds for the public sector while avoiding an unpalatable increase in direct activities on the part of the national government.

A preelection task force appointed by President Johnson and headed by Joseph A. Pechman produced a report late in 1964 that elaborated the revenue-sharing idea. Perhaps because of petulance over advance leaking of the Pechman report contents, or for other reasons, Johnson never released the report and never publicly further espoused revenue sharing. In 1965, a liberal Republican group, the Ripon Society, adopted the concept of revenue sharing, and the bipartisan Advisory Commission on Intergovernmental Relations strongly recommended the use of revenue sharing in a 1967 report.

By the time that President Nixon was inaugurated, revenue sharing had also been endorsed by such members of the intergovernmental lobby as the National Conference of

Governors, the National Conference of Mayors, the National Conference of State Legislative Leaders, and the National Association of Counties. As part of his call for a "New Federalism," President Nixon in August 1969 made his first major appeal for a revenue-sharing program in a special message to Congress. His proposal resulted in no hearings by the appropriate committees there, however, and it appeared to have a very low priority among administration plans.

Nineteen hundred and seventy-one was to be a different story. The President made revenue sharing, in a vastly expanded form, a very major item in his State of the Union address.[2] This time there was no shortage of attention—although the most important attention was negative. Representative Wilbur Mills, then chairman of the House Ways and Means Committee, immediately announced his adamant opposition and promised to hold hearings for the purpose of killing the plan. During the spring and summer of 1971, Nixon and Mills jockeyed for political advantage, with the former Arkansas legislator fairly certain to scuttle the President's program but perhaps in the end likely to come up with a revenue-sharing plan specifically for the cities. By August 1971, the new "battle plan" for price-wage stability had preempted all of the President's attention to economic policy, and he deferred until 1972 the fight for revenue sharing.

Revenue sharing was thus first introduced into Congress by a Republican legislator; then advocated and developed by an economist high in the councils of two Democratic Presidents' administrations; increasingly endorsed by legislators and national associations of government officials on a nonpartisan basis; and, finally, it became a major plank in the "must" legislative list of a Republican president. What is the source of this extraordinary political sex appeal? How did liberals and conservatives, states' righters and federalists come to push an identical program?

The Case for Revenue Sharing

The case for GRS has shifted since 1972 from rational economic arguments and ideological justifications to basic political and self-interested pronouncements; specifically, subnational elected officials enjoy receiving an automatic, limited-strings check each quarter. As we will see below, the political advantages of GRS at the local level are impressive from a local politician's point of view. In short, prepassage arguments have now been tempered by eight years of an ever-increasing dependency on GRS by state and local governments. However, it would be helpful to review briefly a few of the 1972 arguments in support of the concept of GRS and try to anticipate additional ones to be made at renewal time. It is possible to conceptualize the case for GRS in a three-part argument: economic needs, pragmatic considerations, and normative political theory.

THE ECONOMIC CASE

The economic arguments in favor of continuing GRS revolve around the points elaborated in chapter 3. Subnational general-purpose governments need additional funds to meet their domestic duties, and the federal government is blessed with a superior tax structure. The simple remedy then is to continue to transfer federal revenues to subnational jurisdictions in need.

Saddled with high inflation and unemployment in the 1970s, subnational officials pointed out that there was then even greater justification for this fiscal transfer than the late sixties, when GRS first came seriously to the attention of Congress. The poignant case of New York City is not an anomaly of the fiscal health of older urban centers: One can look anywhere in the country and find mini–New Yorks. Examples are Cleveland's fiscal crisis in 1978, Philadelphia's difficulties in financing municipal services, and the high level of fiscal deterioration in older suburban jurisdictions and middle-size midwestern towns.

This trend is hardly new. Since the early 1960s, a powerful economic current has pulled employment and population growth from older northeastern–north central metropolitan centers to the recently developing southern and western regions.[3] Although the employment base in the United States (employees in nonagricultural jobs) increased 46.6 percent from 1960 through 1975, the growth was polarized by a series of regional shifts. The South and West captured nearly 70 percent of this national growth in jobs. Indeed, by 1975 the South had become the nation's center of new employment opportunities. Especially hard hit were the northeastern and north central regions of the country: These lost 936,000 and 500,000 manufacturing jobs respectively from 1970 to 1975. While manufacturing jobs have been declining nationally for some time now, they are still an important source of employment for the northeastern–north central regions.

When one looks at population changes, the result is the same: a net loss for the northeastern and north central regions and a dramatic gain for the South and West. The national population expanded by 18.8 percent from 1960 to 1975. At the same time, northeastern and north central states grew by 10.7 and 11.7 percent respectively, while the South and West grew by 23.9 and 35.0 percent. There are also a number of subregional variations on this theme. Older metropolitan areas are losing both jobs and population, leading to a decline of central cities and older suburbs. Cumulatively, this leads to a loss of the more affluent middle-class taxpayers, semiskilled jobs for the poor, and a tax base for municipal services. In light of this so-called "Snowbelt" decline and "Sunbelt" growth, GRS is an important source of added revenue and flexibility for many subnational governments. GRS meets the needs of growth-oriented subnational governments in their expansion of public goods and services for booming populations, and it helps declining subnational governments manage through this transition period. When this coalition is put together it presents Congress with some very powerful arguments for GRS.

THE PRAGMATIC CASE

The pragmatic case for GRS is somewhat more complex and less straightforward. It involves a criticism of the federal grant-in-aid system. Federal grant restrictions—especially as tied to categorical grants—limit the flexibility of state and local governments to design programs specifically tailored to meet their own needs. A major complaint of smaller jurisdictions and nonmetropolitan governments is that Washington usually designs grants with an eye toward larger urban social problems. Therefore many subnational governments that contract with the federal government are forced to implement programs that are not designed to solve *their* problems. What may be appropriate for Newark may not work at all in a city with a population of 25,000. Second, grantsmanship difficulties, matching requirements, overlapping grants, delays, grants not renewed—all of these frustrate subnational planning, coordination and local governments' ability to deliver the "goods" to their constituents.

A third criticism focuses on the problems of administering federal grants and the "hidden"costs associated with securing federal funding. Jeffrey Pressman and Aaron Wildavsky have documented the administrative costs, political bargaining, and difficulty of implementing federal grants. We have learned from their insightful case study, and those of others, that even with the best intentions at the federal, state, and local levels, it is all but impossible to implement federal guidelines locally without paying a very heavy administrative price.[4] In what could be called the *implementation factor,* a combination of administrative delays and political infighting is bound to result from the multiplicity of actors, interest groups, and confusion over federal intentions.

In another study, Pressman has painted a picture of why implementation factors extract a heavy cost.[5] He points to the stereotypical images intergovernmental actors have of each other. For example, federal officials perceive "locals" to be provincial, narrow-minded, and overtly political in their choice of program priorities. Consequently, they conceptualize federal guidelines as a vehicle to push recalcitrant local governments into the twentieth-century intergovernmental system. Locals, on the other hand, view federal officials and their guidelines as obstacles to be gotten around. The feds are too far away to understand local problems; thus the best one can do is fudge here and there to ensure that local problems are addressed based on a local understanding of the issue.

The result of this oversimplification of intentions and behavior is a series of constantly changing administrative rulings, implemented through a number of actors and multiple "clearance points." The results are high administrative overhead and, at best, long and costly delays. GRS returns administrative, fiscal, and political flexibility to subnational governments. By reducing federal involvement via pragmatic guidelines, subnational governments can plan and coordinate programs that fit pressing needs *as they perceive them.* Funds are forthcoming automatically with a minimum of red tape and in a form clearly designed to improve the implementation process at the subnational level. GRS, it is argued, strikes an equitable balance between sound administrative practices for monitoring from above and the lessons of pragmatic administrative considerations.

There is also dissatisfaction with the results of past federal categorical grants closely monitored by Washington. This is illustrated by the rather severe criticisms of the Johnson administration's "war on poverty" programs in the middle 1960s. This era of American federalism, as noted earlier, was called *creative federalism* and was a time of rapid proliferation of categorical federal grants, primarily targeted to older urban areas that were densely populated pockets of high unemployment and poverty. By most accounts (although these will be challenged below), these federal programs failed to place the unemployed in meaningful jobs or to reduce inner city poverty. The only tangible results of a $2 billion war on poverty were administrative chaos, frustration (on the part of both intended beneficiaries and middle-class taxpayers), and ever-escalating implementation costs. GRS proponets contend that it would be best to allow subnational officials to tend their own gardens. Obviously, even when the feds operate with the best of intentions, the national level is not the appropriate level at which to solve urban problems.

THE POLITICAL ARGUMENT

Finally, the political base of support for GRS and its continuation can be found in normative assertions about the ideals of American federalism.

In recent years, some academics and subnational officials have feared the post–New Deal federal government has usurped too many subnational prerogatives and powers.[6] This centralizing shift has turned state and local governments into handmaidens of the central government. Local control, state determination, regional experimentation, and cultural diversity—not to mention participation—have been given a back seat in the last 25 years.

Concurrent with these fears of turning American federalism into a unitary state, which recent public opinion polls reflect, are economic arguments that point out the limits of centralization. Political economists have for a number of years maintained that administrative centralization is not as efficient, economical, or responsive to the wishes of the citizenry as decentralized units of government.[7]

Taken as a challenge to "creeping centralization," this view provides a normative foundation for GRS. Its proponents, along with those of the financial and pragmatic arguments, pulled together a liberal-conservative coalition in Congress that passed the State and Local Assistance Act of 1972. In 1976, Congress renewed GRS through 1980 along the same lines of support. Subnational governments had become dependent on GRS, and the overriding argument for its renewal in 1976 was fiscal need in times of high unemployment and inflation. Liberals saw GRS (like federal grants-in-aid) as a way to increase public expenditures, but without the political opposition to increasing the federal deficit. Conservatives tend to use GRS more as a way of continuing the substitution of "few strings" federal money for regressive property tax funds rather than as a source for a net increase of federal expenditures.

However, the intergovernmental lobby applied tremendous political pressure in 1972 and 1976 to pass and renew GRS, which by 1976 had become a staple in all receiving jurisdictions' budgets. Regardless of the flaws in its design, one should not minimize the power of these groups over congressional appropriations. In the last analysis, one can attribute GRS less to clearly thought-through positions and more to the power of subnational elected and appointed officials and their urge to keep what they have. GRS now enjoys "incumbency" status and is no longer simply a policy "contender."

The Case Against GRS

There are three serious flaws to the argument that subnational governments are fiscally strapped. First, not all subnational governments exploit their potential revenue sources fully. This is especially true if one looks at comparative state tax efforts. ACIR has pointed out that state income tax rates vary. A typical family in 1974 with an income of $17,500 paid more than $1,000 in Minnesota for its state income tax bite, while for the same family five other states extracted from $801 to $611. At the low end, six states required only $200, and nine states do not levy any income tax. Moreover, there are gross discrepancies between states over what constitutes taxable income, and a number of states give preferential tax rates to industry and capital gains. In short, if all states are in desperate fiscal need (an assumption behind transferring federal revenue to every state capital), then why such inconsistencies?

Second, since 1973, state tax increases have become increasingly rare. In 1977, only Nebraska and Maryland increased their state sales taxes; 2 states raised income taxes; and 4 raised corporate tax rates. Eight states hiked their motor gas taxes.[8] This still leaves 34 supposedly needy states with the status quo!

Finally, because of inflation, a majority of the states found themselves with a very comfortable surplus at the end of 1977. The *National Journal* reported in 1978 that 40 states had combined surpluses of $5.4 billion.[9] The growth states in the Sunbelt were especially flush in 1977, but even a number of Snowbelt states experienced a surplus: New Jersey had one equal to 7 percent of its spending.[10] California alone had a GRS allocation in 1977 of $710.3 million while showing a $6- to $8-billion surplus. It should be noted that state and local surpluses can be explained by a combination of inflation pushing up prices (sales taxes) and wages and salaries (income taxes), and the recession of 1973–1975 postponing needed state capital expenditures, but these figures still point to a glaring flaw in the fiscal need argument. Not all state and local governments are in the red, but GRS goes to *all* general-purpose governments. The GRS distribution formula (discussed below) rewards both the rich and poor, healthy economies and those fiscally depressed, and general-purpose governments with effective tax rates and those that have weak ones. (Changes in fiscal health can come quickly, however: By spring 1979, there was a net nationwide state government deficit of over $6 billion.)

Congressman Ulmer predicted a few years ago that three of the largest expenditure categories for local governments— education, highways, and welfare—can be expected to decline radically.[11] The "postwar baby boom" has tapered off, and there are signs that families in the future will be smaller. Consequently, the demand for new capital expenditures, increased maintenance, and personnel costs in the area of public education should abate. The interstate highway system is about 90-percent completed, and environmentalists will pressure subnational officials to reallocate highway funds. The recent use of the once sacred highway trust fund for mass transportation projects is a good example of this pressure. Although the dollar amount for alternative modes of transportation is still relatively insignificant, the future dominance of personal highway transportation has been questioned.[12]

Lastly, it may be only a few years until we will see the federal government nationalize the financing of welfare. The ill-fated Nixon plan for a guaranteed income was a step in this direction. If states, and especially cities, are relieved of the financial burden of their welfare constributions, their fiscal viability should improve.

While there is no doubt that many local governments—in particular big cities—are struggling with high levels of poverty, unemployment, substandard housing, and a shrinking tax base, it is not true for all local governments. States with huge surpluses could help local governments in need, as California did in 1978–1979 and 1979–1980. By distributing funds to every qualified general-purpose government, GRS spreads scarce resources too thinly. If there is a role for the federal government in helping distressed jurisdictions, it is one of "targeting" scarce dollars to areas that have real need.

The pragmatic case for GRS is weak on a number of other points. There are many administrative problems in the federal grant-in-aid system, especially relating to categorical grants. Federal guidelines are restrictive; multiple actors in the implementation process cause delays, jack up administrative overhead, and frustrate coordination at times. However, one needs an historical understanding of the issue to gain a balanced perspective.

It has long been accepted that subnational governments have been the weakest link in the federal system. Analysts who favor a stronger state-local role in the intergovernmental system have agreed that the states have been lax in developing a modern interstate intergovernmental system in their own jurisdictions.[13] Burdened by ineffective leadership, conservative legislatures, antiquated constitutions that limit local governmental powers, inadequate fiscal specialization, and a history of what can be called antiurban bias, the states have been slow to accept twentieth-century federalism.

Press and Adrian argued nearly 14 years ago that this combination has inhibited state capitals from carrying out their duties responsibly.

We charge that the ideas dominant among the decision makers for state governments lack timeliness. By this we mean that the ideology to which decision makers are beholden is not appropriate as a yardstick against which to judge proposed public policies for today because it is for a rural, small town, preindustrial society rather than for our contemporary urban society.[14]

With few exceptions, which we shall discuss below, their analysis still holds true today.

Furthermore, state capitals have been extremely reluctant to address big city problems. Where state decision makers have actively developed programs, big city interests usually were not uppermost in their minds. As Daniel Grant points out:

> Even where there has been an apparent response by the state to urban pressure for help, the state seems to have been unaware that many of its actions in reality complicate the overall urban problem rather than alleviate it. . . . It does not seem unfair to say that state government decision makers have not really been sufficiently interested.[15]

To quote Adrian again:

> It is probably fair to conclude that state governments are not crippled by general government action nearly so much as they are by their own failure to modernize.[16]

While the full development of this argument would take us beyond the scope of this book, we can examine a short list of structural inadequacies:

1. As of 1978, only three state constitutions permitted deficit financing. Consequently, 47 states cannot plan beyond the current fiscal year and are at the mercy of fluctuations in the national economy.
2. Several state constitutions do not allow the governor to run for a second term. By the time a governor has mastered the office, the term is up.

94

3. A number of state legislatures do not meet in regular session every year. When they do meet, one can hardly expect their members to give primary attention to the job when they are often paid on the assumption that it is a sideline to a career as a lawyer, real estate or insurance dealer, or farmer.

4. Ten states have the term of governor fixed at two years—hardly enough time to take command of the office. Moreover, a number of states deliberately weaken the governor's office by independently electing top state officials who are not fully responsible to the governor (e.g., lieutenant governors, superintendents of education, controllers, etc.).

5. Until quite recently, a majority of states did not attract or pay for first-rate talent at the state level. As a result, a political vacuum was created into which flowed the lobbyists for special business interests. If the government leaders are incapable of leading, private leaders are more than willing to pick up the ball and run with it.

It seems fair to conclude that there are inherent problems in the administration of state government.

But a balanced picture requires some mention of recent changes in this gloomy analysis. Several states can be singled out as models of dramatic improvement in state government, and state government is generally more professional, environmentally aware, planning-oriented, and fiscally responsive than a generation ago. In particular, state aid to local governments has expanded and taken on a new significance. For example, in 1954 state capitals provided $5.7 billion in direct local aid, close to 40 percent of what local governments raised on their own. By 1975, state aid rose to $50.5 billion or about 60 percent of the local effort. The additional help allows local governments to depend less on the regressive local property tax. However, over half of state aid still goes to education, and less than 3 percent of state aid in 1975 was targeted for urban services.[17]

In addition to their expanding fiscal role, a number of states are eliminating unnecessary red tape, upgrading their civil service systems, and introducing economy and efficiency techniques into the administration of their governments. Colorado's attempts to implement sunset legislation, Georgia's much-heralded zero-base budgeting, and California's mental health reforms are but a few examples of efforts to improve state bureaucracies.

Historically, state capitals have promoted metropolitan balkanization, sprawl, and transportation networks that have drained older big cities (the federal government is the villain here as well). They have also turned a deaf ear toward the pleas of big city mayors for increased state aid and legislation that might halt the decline of big cities. There are now signals from a few state capitals that this is changing. Massachusetts and Michigan can be cited for a new urban awareness. Both states, under strong executive leadership, have embarked on a new era of state–big city relations. Under the Dukakis administration, Massachusetts began to target state facilities, redirect public works, and increase state aid to densely populated areas, and state policy favored the rehabilitation of older downtown facilities, as opposed to new construction. Massachusetts instituted a new loan program to aid private firms that stayed in or located in the central cities and took a number of steps to reverse the fiscal drain on older larger cities. As a result, in 1976 about one third of the state's new industrial jobs were in the cities as opposed to the suburbs.[18]

Michigan's approach has been less comprehensive and is primarily concerned with economic development. Detroit, a city that a number of urbanologists had given up as a wasteland, is beginning to show signs of new life. Governor Milliken has changed state aid formulas to increase Detroit's share of funds. Through a property tax abatement plan, the Chrysler Corporation kept a large facility in Detroit and invested over $100 million in plant renovation. City revenue increased and 5,000 jobs were saved.[19] A unique component of Michigan's new economic development approach is the concept of an *equity payment* ($30 million alone in 1977 to Detroit) to defray the costs of providing services for suburbanites. Examples are increased police costs for traffic control, at cultural events, road maintenance costs, health, and transportation.[20]

California's urban strategy, Minnesota's Twin Cities, Metropolitan Regional Council, and Albany's new concern with New York City are also good examples of improved state performance. On the whole, though, state government has a long way to go in developing a modern intergovernmental machine. A few examples here and there do not mean that the 50 state capitals can be counted on to assume new responsibilities on their own, and "few strings" aid, such as GRS, is not calculated to provide the incentives—the leverage—needed to move more states toward more rapid modernization. GRS could, however, be amended in that direction.

The recent improvement in performance on the part of a growing number of states can clearly be attributed to the federal "carrot and stick" approach. Advances in state support for depressed jurisdictions, social services, environmental protection, planning, and coordination are direct results of stimulus attached to many federal grant-in-aid programs. Examples here include the Office of Management and Budget's circular A-95, which requires state and regional area-wide planning and review before grants were funded for a large number of federal programs, and the "701 planning assistance program," which provides the impetus for a number of states to develop effective planning departments. As this was written, the efforts of the Environmental Protection Agency and President Carter's national urban policy directives were nudging states into new planning coordination and assistance programs.

In short, it took federal leverage to shake up state capitals and stimulate reform. While it is true that the administrative costs of the carrot and stick approach have been high and have hampered the success of many programs, the alternatives, given state history, are few. We may find that the costs incurred have been worth it (especially concerning domestic R&D) when a twenty-first century analyst reviews federal efforts since the 1960s. GRS, it must be remembered, is based on the philosophy that federal policy involvement should be kept to a minimum. Consequently, it attenuates the long and tortuous federal effort to engender greater responsibility in state capitals.

Several other complaints of subnational governments should also be critically reviewed. It is argued that the subnational matching requirement diverts priorities, especially at the local level. However, the issue is more complex than this. Federal aid—including GRS—is nationally collected revenue. The matching requirement promotes subnational spending and is intended to prevent subnational governments from using federal funds as a substitution for their own tax efforts and revenues. Federal aid should be additive in that it stimulates additional state-local effort; encouraging substitution would contribute a major (and never consciously articulated and debate) departure from the goals of the federal aid system as designed over the years.

A study at Syracuse University's Maxwell Graduate School of Citizenship and Public Affairs analyzed how well the federal matching requirement met this goal. It found that matching requirements stimulate subnational expenditures, and the higher the match, the higher the stimulation. When the match was lower, the level of stimulation was also lower.[21] There seems to be a correlation between federal specificity in terms of a subnational fiscal commitment and the stimulation of expenditures in a given functional area (an area, it should be noted, that previously was supported at a much lower level).

By not requiring matching funds, the federal government allows national revenue to be used as a substitute for subnational revenue. GRS, as we will see below, does not require a match, nor, with few exceptions, does it stimulate new subnational spending on national social problems.

What has been called the problem of proliferation of grants actually may increase choice rather than stifle creativity. Local governments can pick and choose among the 400 or so federal grants. The overlapping of grants has been simplified since 1974, through the trend toward block grants (discussed in the next chapter). Since most of these new block grants are based on automatic eligibility formulas, this trend reduces the problem of grantsmanship.

The political nature of federal grants, however, has not changed. Rather, the focus of intense political activity has now shifted from competitive grantsmanship to influencing the design of the formula and the weight given to formula variables. A change in one variable can mean a difference of millions of dollars to specific jurisdictions. For example, if poverty and the age of housing are double weighted, older cities would receive a substantial windfall. On the other hand, if median income and new growth are built in, the South and new suburbs would qualify for additional aid at the expense of older cities in the Northeast. The key point here is that decentralizing federal aid by automatic eligibility formulas does not neutralize the politics of federal aid—it just shifts the arena.

In summary, the pragmatic arguments over the hardening of categories, proliferation of grants, implementation obstacles, etc., are real but exaggerated. In the intergovernmental system there are many points of access, and the system is replete with "intergovernmental diplomacy." Federal aid through the carrot and stick approach has helped to stimulate subnational modernization. Subnational actors have influence over the type of aid available, the amount allocated to a particular program in a given fiscal year, and how the guidelines will be drawn up.

The Values of Decentralization

The last and perhaps most compelling justification, at least rhetorically, for the New Federalism concerns a normative preoccupation with the values of decentralization. It seems to be axiomatic in some quarters that strengthening the hands of state and local governments will restore American federalism to the form designed by the founding fathers. Wrapped up in the clichés of "power to the people," "community control," "representative democracy," or "increased participation" is an unquestioned assumption that democracy (usually left undefined) is best stimulated by having power returned to the grass roots.

A more moderate faction of this school argues for a stronger state role in the intergovernmental system and a return of unconditional federal revenue to the local level. Basically, this point of view regards the states as laboratories and a healthy component of a vibrant federal system. There are three basic questions in this line of argumentation. First, to what extent can one rely on the experimental thesis in a complex intergovernmental world? Second, is it true that an increase in federal influence will be at the expense of subnational governments—a zero-sum analogy? Third, and most basic, is American democratic theory violated by the national government's involvement in substate activities? This is a test of the "closer to the people" argument in American thought. Each of these ideas will be briefly developed in turn.

The notion of the states as laboratories makes a good deal of sense for the initial experimentation, but the value of the experiment is maximized if the power of national government disseminates the successful innovation to the rest of the states. To rely upon 49 state legislatures to learn about the successes and failures of the fiftieth is to rely on a will-o'-the wisp. Alice Rivlin points out that we learned a great deal about what and where the problems are, their magnitude, and what works or fails in the flurry of experimentation in the 1960s. Now is the time, she believes, for systematic experimentation—as opposed to random ad hoc experiments—if we are to address social problems head on.[22] State experimentation combined with national action, ranging from the inducement of federal grants through state actions mandated by the national government to programs directly operated by the national government, is the appropriate combination. As we noted earlier, the most innovative social and planning experimentation of recent years has come from *federal* stimulus. To rely on any other alternative is to fly by the seat of the pants.

As to the second point, paradoxical though it may seem, it is possible to argue that subnational and in particular state power expand with national expansion. If we view policy-making power as a fixed pie divided into components (say two-fourths federal, one-fourth state, and one-fourth local), the expansion of one level would be at the expense of another. But the expansion of the national government's role does not fit such an analogy. As two recent analysts state:

> The growth of national power is hardly open to argument; but the loss of state power is subject to debate. Although some commentators and politicians regard the expansion of the national role as being at the expense of the state, the fact is that the states, too, are doing more, spending more, and employing more people, and so are local governments. If the total functions of American government are viewed as fixed, an increase in the portion of one government automatically decreases the shares of others. If, on the other hand, governmental functions are viewed as undergoing expansion at all levels, this may not necessarily be true. . . . We believe this is what is happening in the United States: The powers of all governments are increasing.[23]

The last point to be taken up is the argument that the preservation of American democracy and accountability to "the people" by elected officials are best ensured at the local level. Supposedly state and local officials will often have a better sense and appreciation of local values.

Let's stop and look at that for a minute. Are they closer to the people? In what sense? What kind of closeness is meant? Closer to all the people in their respective jurisdictions, or to certain categories of politically effective people?

For many of the poor, and for non-Anglo racial and ethnic groups, closeness is debatable. These groups have long struggled even to be acknowledged, let alone have influence, at the subnational level. If one looks at civil rights efforts— including the women's movement—one finds that state and especially local governments had to be pushed into making minimal efforts to guarantee basic rights. Pushed, that is, by the federal government, which gave a far better response than did local governments and state capitals.

Thus closeness is no guarantee of responsiveness. If the slogan of "power to the people" has taught us anything, it is that it operationally means power to *some* of the people—which ones being dependent on the social and political structure of an area. For every state that tries to address the problems of minority groups—a recent example would be California and the migrant farm workers—there are other states which, in the name of local control, ignore company towns that suspend civil rights. Closeness also can mean the close supervision of groups that want a better shake in life from the public sector. Most proponents of local control turn a deaf ear toward this kind of evidence, which points to the provincial and at times brutal side of community control. A further elaboration on this theme will be developed when we review the impact of GRS spending patterns on local services.

To conclude, the "pro and con" arguments in the prepassage debate over GRS (certain to be raised again in the 1980 renewal process) set up the issues by which to assess the system. GRS can be thought to have four goals. First, to strengthen subnational officials in their roles as policy makers. Second, to improve subnational revenue systems with added money to expand services or help local governments in declining regions. Third, to provide additional resources for state and local governments to experiment with, based on their perceptions of their problems. Lastly, to increase local participation in the decision-making process. In assessing the impact of GRS on the four goals we now turn to its actual pattern of use. What have subnational governments been doing with GRS since 1973? What have been the successes and problems to date? More important, what has been the fate of a major intended thrust of the New Federalism—its efforts to decentralize the intergovernmental system and limit federal programmatic authority.

The Mechanical Issues: How GRS Works

Before reviewing the actual impact of GRS as an alternative model of fiscal federalism, we will mention briefly a few "nuts and bolts" dimensions of how GRS is distributed and the problems of federal aid by formula. GRS is allocated by a formula that divides a fixed sum of money among all general-purpose governments. A simple idea at first blush, it is far more complicated than meets the eye. There are over 2000,000 pieces of governmental financial and socioeconomic data used to compute individual entitlements.[24] There are different formulas for states than there are for intrastate distributions. The formula, which was put into operation in 1973 (and is basically the same in the 1976 amendments), is a House and Senate compromise that takes into account such variables as population, relative income, tax effort, and urbanized population. One third goes to state capitals and two thirds to local general-purpose governments. While this is a simplistic overview, the important point is that for the intergovernmental aid to best respond to our needs as a nation, the above variables ought to build in fiscal need and provide automatically for the targeting of additional resources based on state and local needs.

However, this is not the case. When Congress was considering the formula issues, numerous political interests came to the fore to lobby for variables (and their relative weights) that would benefit one jurisdiction at the expense of another. Pitted against each other were big city vs. suburban interests, southern vs. northern regional interests, small city vs. middle-size city interests, and so on. The result was a formula compromise so complex that in 1976 even big city officials (who complained of being short-changed) dared not agitate for revisions. To open up the can of worms again would be to chance losing what one already could count on. The stakes are high, with approximately $56 billion in GRS having been distributed from 1972 through 1980.

As mentioned earlier, federal aid by formula does introduce political decisions. The types of variables used and their relative weighting have very important consequences for the allocation of scarce federal resources. The GRS formula gives an edge to smaller jurisdictions and suburbs while slighting larger urban governments. First of all, GRS is a *distributive* fiscal policy, as opposed to redistributive. Some funds go to *every* eligible general-purpose government, based on poverty, population, or current fiscal health. This spreading effect waters down the whole pot, imposing artificial limits on aid to fiscally depressed jurisdictions. Second, while big cities, poorer jurisdictions, and large urban areas receive the largest amount of aid per capita, their needs are proportionately even greater than those of many general-purpose governments currently receiving a quarterly check. A recent Brookings Institution study puts the problem succinctly: "The problems of the most troubled central cities are not in any major way ameliorated by general revenue sharing."[25]

The fiscal problems of American cities are far from homogeneous in origin, symptoms, or cures. Since the GRS formula rewards everyone, it precludes the possibility of targeting by need the special circumstances. The majority of receiving jurisdictions are very small, with four fifths under 5,000 in population.[26] Since they only receive 5 percent of the total GRS pot, the dollar amount is not large. But 5 percent of the $55.8 billion sent to subnational governments translates into $2.79 billion that was not available for jurisdictions in greater fiscal difficulty.

In order to continue to receive GRS every quarter, receiving jurisdictions must comply with several procedural and programmatic guidelines. First, GRS funds cannot be used to support any activities that discriminate by age, handicap, religion, race, color, national origin, or sex. This nondiscrimination provision was considerably strengthened in the 1976 amendments. A recipient jurisdiction must prove by "clear and convincing" evidence that GRS has not funded all or part of a program or activity that is not in compliance with the civil rights guidelines. However, GRS can *indirectly* support such programs and activities, as we will explore below. Second, in 1976 the public participation requirements were also strengthened. Unless waived by the Secretary of the Treasury, recipient governments must hold two public hearings on GRS. The first, held before the budget is presented to the governing body, sets forth its proposed use; the second allows citizens to voice their opinions on how GRS should be used in relation to the recipient government's entire budget.

In the original revenue-sharing act, recipient governments were only to spend their entitlements in specific priority categories. Because the requirement was difficult to monitor (discussed below), it was dropped in the 1976 amendments, along with the provision against using GRS in any form as part of a recipient's match for a categorical grant. Now receiving jurisdictions can use GRS for any activity they please, specifically including use as their match for a federal categorical grant.

In addition to the above provisions in the 1972 act and 1976 amendments, recipient governments must at the end of each fiscal year submit to the Treasury Department a report "setting forth the amounts and purposes for which funds . . . have been appropriated, spent, or obligated . . . and showing the relationship of these funds to the relevant functional items in the government's budget. Such report shall identify differences between the actual use of funds received and proposed use of such funds."[27] Also, ten days before the public hearings on the budget are held, they must publish in at least one newspaper with a general circulation the proposed uses of GRS funds with a summary of the proposed budget. Recipient governments are not required to publish the adopted budget or the adopted uses of GRS. Under the law they are only to make available such material for public inspection thirty days after the budget is adopted. The last major provision requires that recipient jurisdiction adhere to the Davis-Bacon Act that defines the prevailing wage rates in cases where more than 25 percent of the total costs of a capital project are funded by revenue sharing.

It should now be clear that the procedural and programmatic guidelines are considerably weaker than the ones used for categorical and block grants. The difficulties of monitoring and ensuring compliance and the impact of this significant shift in decentralization will be discussed later. But for now the point is that the Office of Revenue Sharing in the Treasury Department loosely monitors about 39,000 recipient jurisdictions ranging from an entitlement of only $200 to several million dollars a quarter. Laboring with a small staff (at this writing about 200) and limited in its authority to interview, the Office of Revenue Sharing in effect leaves it up to the good intentions of recipient governments to stay within the spirit of the law and use GRS for worthwhile projects. As a National Science Foundation study concluded, for "the first time in the history of federal domestic assistance, all general purpose governments are eligible recipients, and receive entitlements. . . . There is no precedent for a federal grant program of the size of GRS that relies solely on data for the determination of allocations."[28] Keeping this in mind, let us review the "actual use pattern" of revenue sharing.

GRS: An Expenditure Review and Assessment

Three remarks should be made before we look at the actual use pattern of GRS. First, the reports filed with the Office of Revenue Sharing are not good indicators of how GRS is being spent. The problem is one of *fungibility*, a term economists use to describe the interchangeability of money. GRS funds that are allocated for a particular use may free up funds that without revenue sharing would have been assigned to that function. Thus the newly liberated funds can be used by the recipient government for other purposes that are *not* reported to Washington. This difficulty makes the reporting data very weak indeed—as we will see below. Second, at this writing the major monitoring studies cover the use and impact of GRS only up to July 1975. There may have been shifts in the allocation of revenue-sharing funds by the time the reader reviews the analysis below. However, we believe it to be most unlikely that changes will undermine our analysis of the impact of GRS or the decentralizing assumptions of the New Federalism. Third, and most important, since GRS is a distributive policy spread over 39,000 jurisdictions, any ultimate judgment of its success or failure will inevitably involve some normative judgments: Revenue sharing means different things to different people. Therefore our criteria will have to be clearly spelled out.

Deil Wright believes that three approaches have been used to study the impact of revenue sharing:

1. the official actual and planned use reports filed by recipient governments with the Office of Revenue Sharing;
2. observer research case studies and comparative analyses;
3. participant-observer perceptions or perspectives.[29]

The first approach, as already noted, is not reliable because of the fungibility issue. The second, while relying on representative samples, is the most systematic and objective. The third is subjective, sometimes ideologically skewed, and lacks a balanced analysis. Therefore we will rely primarily on the second approach in explaining the impacts of GRS. Two of the largest and most impressive monitoring projects have been conducted by the Brookings Institution and the National Science Foundation (NSF).[30] The major Brookings study, until 1979 under the direction of economist Richard Nathan, has been monitoring revenue sharing since its inception. The research of the NSF study was conducted prior to July 1975 and is based mainly on the earliest years of revenue sharing. Between these and other sources, we can piece together the revenue-sharing picture and assess the impact of the most controversial part of the New Federalism.

If we review the arguments in support of revenue sharing and Congressional hearings, we can analyze the four over-arching goals GRS is to meet. As we shall see, GRS has fallen quite short of the mark. Weak performance on the part of subnational recipients calls into question the axiom of the New Federalism that the states and local governments know what is needed and how best to address major social ills in their own jurisdictions. This assessment will be examined below.

DECISION MAKING AND PARTICIPATION

Proponents of GRS hoped and argued that it would increase participation and strengthen the policy choices of political generalists at the local level. If new funds were available at the state and especially local level, then the grass-roots model of American politics would provide the democratic give and take that allows citizens to mobilize and lobby their respective elected officials. In turn, political generalists would be free to respond to their wishes, instead of being the handmaidens of the federal government. Moreover, GRS would stimulate a new (revived?) interest in the local budget; its priorities and expenditures. Thus a balance could be struck between federal and grass-roots preferences.

But we find that after the initial flurry of activity that GRS caused at the local level (the impact of new funds midyear after the 1973 budget had been adopted), there was a return to the generally apathetic status quo. The Brookings studies and an independent General Accounting Office study confirm this. What GRS did stimulate, apparently in a lasting way, is greater participation on the part of special interest groups (e.g., local agencies, public works, private charitable agencies, chambers of commerce, and former poverty program clientele groups) wanting a piece of the local revenue-sharing pie. Many of these groups have always had more leverage at the subnational—particularly local—level, and this fact may have discouraged the average citizen from competing for attention. This, coupled with the fact that GRS does not explicitly require citizen participation, limits grass-roots involvement.

A number of jurisdictions have established citizen advisory groups to help legislative bodies set priorities for revenue-sharing projects. However, this institutionalized response to promoting representative democracy is uneven. One study three years after revenue sharing began found that only 17.2 percent of cities and 25.8 percent of counties had established advisory groups. Larger urban areas fared much better, especially for cities over 300,000.[31] Still, the uneven response undermines the hopes that GRS would stimulate a new participatory era. In fact, the National Clearinghouse on Revenue Sharing reported in 1975:

Citizen advisory groups, even where they exist, have little real power. Their function may be to make recommendations for allocating a limited amount of money among many claimants—thus relieving public officials of the political burden inherent in such decision-making. . . . Furthermore, advising groups may not be representative of the community as a whole.[32]

It is the opinion of one of the present authors, having served on a local advisory board, that this is indeed the case. If revenue sharing was supposed to strengthen the role of political generalists so that they would have the flexibility to make hard decisions based on increased citizen input, then it has noticeably failed to do so. Of course, citizen and group participation differs by city size, socioeconomic composition, and fiscal health, but on the whole participation is quite limited. Nor has the level of citizen participation increased generally in the preparation of the local budget. In spite of the requirement that two public hearings be held, the level of grass-roots involvement leaves much to be desired.

Turning a critical eye toward state capitals, one finds the same business-as-usual attitude. There are no studies showing that revenue sharing changed the decision-making process at the state level because of increased citizen participation. Governors or state legislatures set spending priorities without much consultation with citizen groups and local government officials.

For example, "Louisiana explicitly earmarked all of its shared revenue [GRS] for highway projects, while Colorado earmarked its shared revenues for offsetting cutbacks in federal categorical grants."[33] In jurisdictions under heavy fiscal pressure, "executive dominance" influenced the allocation of revenue sharing. It is true that jurisdictions facing shrinking resources have little choice but to push through decisions concerning revenue sharing without seriously considering alternatives based on citizen preference. But the case made for GRS—that it would stimulate major changes in subnational decision making—is still undermined. The Brookings monitoring study confirms this position: "It would seem reasonable to conclude that the expectations of some that there would be a dramatic change in the politics of state and local governments as a result of revenue sharing have not been born out."[34]

Another major goal of revenue sharing was to allow recipient governments the flexibility to set their own priorities, develop their own programs, and experiment with innovative ideas based on their understanding of indigenous problems. This goal was established in response to a number of pragmatic grievances with the grant-in-aid system (such as the hardening of the grant "arteries" syndrome) and also in response to "the closer to the problem the better" argument in addressing subnational problems. Moreover, the use of GRS for innovation would support the belief in the states and their respective local governments as experimental laboratories. If GRS was used to modernize local governments, change antiquated structural arrangements, stimulate consolidation of small and overlapping governments, reduce the number of special purpose districts, or stimulate new spending on national problems that manifest themselves locally, then it could be judged a success. Furthermore, GRS could be used as a catalyst for metropolitan planning efforts if any of the above goals were met.

The sparse data so far available, however, indicate that subnational governments have not rushed to develop and support new programs. The main exception has been a tendency of county governments (which were expanding their service role before revenue sharing) to make significant use of GRS for new or expanding operating programs.[35]

When we look at innovative programs or improved delivery of public goods and services, the same can be said. In the areas of new social service delivery systems, community development activities, or public housing, one can seek in vain for a clear pattern of innovative subnational activity. Of course, it can be argued that revenue sharing was thought of initially as a one-time shot in the arm to help subnational governments with the burden of "stagflation." Therefore officials were reluctant to commit GRS to new programs or innovative projects, only to be left holding the bag when it terminated in 1976. But revenue sharing was extended in 1976, and the likelihood of it continuing indefinitely in some form is clearly very strong. The suspect reporting data, and major monitoring studies since 1973, have pointed to an increasing trend not to put GRS to work in new areas but (as we will see below) to merge it into ongoing operating expenditures.

As we turn to possible structural reforms that would modernize state and local governments, a mixed but clearly discernible trend emerges. The second Brookings study perceives "a tendency for the program to reinforce and maintain the position of small and limited-function governmental units in rural (though not urban) areas.[36] However, this interpretation should be amended to include the possibility that GRS also "props up" suburban jurisdictions in older metropolitan areas. Many of these governments have received only limited federal aid in the past. Revenue sharing is the first federal assistance for which a number of them were eligible or had applied for. These suburban governments ring older cities and use their economic bases, services, and cultural activities. Yet because of complex legal and political reasons, they do not contribute to the older cities' tax bases. There is no way of telling how many of these suburban units of government, under the pressures of inflation, were contemplating consolidation with older cities. Revenue-sharing funds now delay the day when they must "bite the bullet" on consolidation. An indirect impact of GRS therefore may be to prop up suburban jurisdictions that strangle older cities by draining off fiscal resources. In sum, GRS does help rural governments to keep afloat and modestly improve their infrastructures, while providing a windfall income that permits suburban jurisdictions to maintain their autonomy.

There is a GRS incentive for smaller jurisdictions to consolidate (i.e., a potential increase in their total allocation under the current formula); but it is a limited incentive because the current statute specifies that the annexed areas must equal at least 5 percent of the annexing unit's population. Few suburban populations equal 5 percent of those of older cities. This requirement, together with formula provisions requiring that no eligible government receive an allotment of less than 20 percent (or more than 145 percent) of the statewide average per capital allotment to local governments, benefits limited-function governments and penalizes larger urban units of government.[37]

The unintended consequence of social action, to paraphrase Robert Merton, may be that revenue sharing (and the New Federalism in general) perpetuates sprawl, fragmentation, and the exploitation of older urban areas. In its present form, GRS does not stimulate much modernization or structural reform, such as consolidation or metropolitan area planning. In fact, there are no requirements or incentives for substate planning or for the evaluation of programs undertaken with federal funds. This point was debated in both the prepassage hearing in 1972 and the 1976 renewal hearings. Congressman Reuss argued in 1971 that GRS should provide incentives for modernization and penalties for jurisdictions that do not implement broad reforms, and Congressman Rosenthal of New York made a similar pitch in 1976. Both proposals were strongly opposed by state and local officials through the intergovernmental lobby.

FISCAL EFFECTS

Since revenue sharing has not stimulated citizen participation, innovation, modernization, or new programs and has not appreciably changed subnational decision-making processes, what has it been used for? And what have been the fiscal effects of revenue sharing at the subnational level?

Again, the results are mixed. In the early years, a number of local governments, especially smaller jurisdictions, put most of their revenue-sharing receipts into one-time capital expenditures such as new courthouses, city halls, and libraries because of the uncertainty of renewal. Most of these capital projects were already on the drawing board, and so local governments *substituted* GRS for their own funds; they thus also avoided the necessity of borrowing through the municipal bond market and stabilized their tax rates. Both effects—substitution of GRS for own source revenue and borrowing avoidance—allow local officials to finance new construction without raising the local property tax or affecting other revenue sources. Since this a very seductive incentive from a local perspective, it is no surprise that early GRS spending on capital expenditures accounted for "a larger appropriation of shared-revenue uses than any other net effect category."[38] On the other hand, hard-pressed jurisdictions with declining central cities were forced to commit revenue sharing for operating expenditures. Because revenue-sharing funds are additive for jurisdictions under light or moderate fiscal pressure, such areas can substitute them for bricks and mortar projects. Older, hard-pressed cities do not have this flexibility, even though they receive a higher entitlement on a per capita base than relatively better-off jurisdictions. This raises serious questions about revenue sharing's distributional effects and social equity. Again, GRS is flawed because of its inability to target resources.

POLITICAL EFFECTS

Two important political effects—one purposeful, the other unanticipated—can be attributed to revenue sharing. The first is a return of clout to political generalists, that is, a return of discretion and policy-making authority to locally elected officials, city managers, county executives, etc. One of the arguments leveled against the federal grant-in-aid system was that functional specialists too often tied the hands of elected officials because of their expertise, grantsmanship, and contacts with other specialists at higher levels in a specific functional area, say manpower or urban renewal. Functional specialists, it was argued, used governing bodies as rubber stamps in approving grant applications and programs. Now GRS money comes to general-purpose governments directly with few procedural strings, allowing political generalists to pick and choose programs and priorities on their own. In trying to secure revenue-sharing funds, functional specialists must now make a case to those elected and responsible to the whole community, not just to their administrative counterparts at the state or federal level. In larger urban areas this shift is modest because of the pressing demands to allocate GRS for operating expenditures. Moreover, larger urban areas also participate in other federal aid programs that carry federal requirements, program choices, and priorities. In smaller jurisdictions under light fiscal pressure, however, there has been a very significant shift; GRS constitutes a larger percentage of their federal aid.

This issue is tied to the trend toward the professionalization of government. Few indeed are the programs that really reflect an electoral will, a response to a "gut feeling" among voters. Our system works much more indirectly, and the major mediators between the people and the policy-making officials of government are the professionals and administrators in each field. For example, public housing is designed not directly in response to the ideas of local or state officials or even the potential occupants, but in accord with the ideas of housing experts and administrators of the Housing and Urban Development Department.

If we return programmatic choice to all eligible subnational officials, can we expect their priorities, choices, ideas, and judgments to reflect professional criteria? Many are part-time officials; others are underpaid if full time; and in smaller nonmetropolitan jurisdictions, they often lack education and experience. A number of "locals" do not understand the interdependencies of our complex society, the need for systematic planning by city and region, nor the strong possibility that their decisions may impose a costly externality payment on the surrounding region. Deeply suspicious of federal red tape, bureaucrats, and federal aid regulations, they are likely to take an "I know best" stance that could result in costly environmental and land-use damage. We also fear that the local decision-making structure often might exclude the "have nots" under the self-justified rationale of a neo–Social Darwinism. Local officials want federal aid (nationally collected revenues) without taking the responsibility for targeting monies for national problems.

It is obvious from the literature that many, perhaps most, local governments—and a number of state governments—do not have the technical capacity to plan effectively, or the political will and structure to pursue new programs aggressively. The New Federalism in many instances just reinforces the local power arrangements. As Jeffrey Pressman says:

> Effective action at the local level can be hampered by the absence of institutions with extensive formal powers, by the lack of a strong and coherent system of parties and gorups, and by timid behavior on the part of elected leaders.

Federal funds can provide additional resources to local leaders, and politically adept local executives have been able to use those resources to their own advantage.[39]

This problem of milking federal aid for personal advancement occurs in all forms of federal assistance. Whether it be urban renewal, public housing, or manpower grants, local and state officials will try to take credit. However, since GRS is a quiet form of revenue transferring, it is not stamped "funding with federal money." Consequently, it has the potential for much greater political mileage. Sarah F. Liebschutz concluded from a study of New York state governments that "revenue-sharing funds did represent a political resource used in various ways by the chief elected official, from specific campaign references to it by Rochester's mayor, to keeping it all quiet: allowing voters to draw their own conclusions about the efficiency of the town supervisors."[40] GRS can benefit incumbents campaigning on a new courthouse, library, or municipal tennis courts and swimming pools—all without borrowing or raising property taxes.

The two political impacts of GRS are questionable. First, it does in varying degrees return power to political generalists. But can they all handle it wisely? Second, the unintended political consequence of GRS is that incumbents receive new resources and are encouraged in political entrepreneurship. Since incumbents have had the edge in subnational and congressional elections anyway, GRS can only add to this head start and reinforce the status quo. These issues will be developed a bit further below when we look at the impact GRS has had on subnational accountability.

THE ACCOUNTABILITY ISSUES

To measure revenue sharing's impact on the accountability dimension, we must necessarily lay out criteria that involve normative judgments. Evaluations of spending patterns, compliance with procedural guidelines (i.e., civil rights), planning activities, etc. require judgments concerning how GRS should be used and what constitutes abuses of the law's intentions. Locally perceived priorities may not meet national goals and address national problems, but is that what the act intended? Perhaps this question assumes that they should, if one damns locals for being provincial.

Our working interpretation is that GRS should be used in ways that benefit the community as a whole, without discriminating against minorities; and that revenue sharing should address national problems—in particular, the needs of the disadvantaged—by funding social services. Many of the federal grants that supported social services have been consolidated (see chapter 5) or phased out in the hopes that GRS would pick up the slack at the state and local levels.

Policy accountability, then, can be defined as the expectation that elected representatives will respond to the needs of their constituents in an honest and open fashion. GRS should increase this local accountability and reach out to groups not particularly well mobilized to make their needs known.

When one looks at the use pattern of GRS—what it bought—at the state and local levels, it is quite clear that social services have not been a high priority. The Brookings study confirms this analysis.

> Our second-round field data indicate that recipient governments have, in fact, put relatively little emphasis on social-service programs. Included under this heading are such activities as legal aid, job training and placement, counseling, and housing assistance. In general, these services are aimed at the aged, low-income groups, and other categories of disadvantaged persons.[41]

119

Only 2 to 4 percent of revenue sharing was allocated by states, counties, and cities for social services. Township governments spent nothing![42] These aggregate figures are subject to a number of regional and substate variations, of course. Moreover, there are a few good examples of revenue sharing expenditures on new or expanded social service programs.[43] Also, we should remember that it is not easy to pinpoint from statistical reports what constitutes a social service: new sidewalks, tax abatement which could help the elderly, or a Head Start program? Still, one can say that subnational governments have not taken an aggressive or even moderately strong role in supporting social service activities with GRS funds.

Accept for the moment that new city swimming pools, libraries, sidewalks, and police cars can be thought of as distributional social services that benefit all constituents in roughly an equal manner. (A large assumption.) It is still important to know the location of these projects, whether access routes favor one income group over another (time, roads, physical obstacles, etc.). To date, we know of no studies that have tried to correlate the location of a project funded by GRS and its possible de facto discrimination. A city swimming pool in a primarily upper-middle-class neighborhood will proportionately benefit those residents more than lower-income residents who have to drive for 20 minutes or so. The same can be said of a city park or new sewer system. Since GRS reinforces the propensity of political generalists to take credit for such projects, they will be tempted to locate them in neighborhoods that have the highest and most consistent voter turnout. Voting studies tell us that the more affluent fit this bill nicely. Without being unduly harsh, we can suspect GRS of increasing the accountability of political generalists to such groups at the expense of others. It would seem that the poor get a better "accountability quotient" from the federal level.

The expanded nondiscrimination provisions in the 1976 amendments reinforce this dilemma. Recipient governments can be held accountable only for "direct" uses of revenue sharing. It is thus very difficult for minorities and other groups to force recipient governments to correct activities that discriminate indirectly, as discussed above. Linked with revenue sharing's fungibility, GRS may perpetuate subtle, legally unreasonable acts of discrimination.

Accountability also should reflect the number of elected and administrative positions occupied by a representative sample of groups in a community. Here is the tricky part: Will revenue sharing lead to the upward mobility of the historically disadvantaged through the expansion of new subnational positions? The fact that GRS favors the retention of incumbents leads one to believe that it will be more difficult to change the faces on a city council.

GRS does strengthen the affirmative action role of the federal government. In one well-publicized case in 1975, the city of Chicago, under a court order, had almost $19 million per quarter of revenue-sharing funds withheld in 1975 because of alleged discrimination in police hiring.[44] Although GRS allows wide latitude in programmatic choice, this does *not* preclude the federal government from enforcing a number of national goals indirectly. However, the Chicago case was a blatant one, and there are over 39,000 recipient governments that may pursue similar policies undetected. The costs, time, and monitoring difficulties make universal compliance all but impossible.

Increased accountability at the subnational level is uneven, precarious, and difficult to measure. But an early analysis indicates that GRS has not stimulated a new accountability toward all groups in a recipient government's jurisdiction.

Accountability also has a fiscal dimension. At a time of a growing national deficit and high unemployment coupled

121

with double digit inflation, scarce national resources should be targeted so as to maximize the greatest good. GRS, as argued previously, separates tax-collecting responsibilities from spending priorities and puts the federal government in the position of allocating funds (at times borrowed against the future) for unspecified priorities. In fact, the difficulties in tracking down just how subnational governments allocate their entitlements (fungibility) raise serious issues about federal accountability in general. Should the federal government use nationally collected resources in ways that are difficult to assess and for purposes that are limited to narrow geographical concerns? We believe that federal accountability mechanisms must be clear and direct; that federal allocations must be targeted for national problem solving (e.g., unemployment, welfare); and that subnational recipients of nationally collected revenue must be accountable to the same goals.

Summary

GRS has not lived up to its stated goals. A "shotgun" approach to federal aid cannot, by its very nature, solve national problems or work toward national goals. It will be hard to reverse the trends of spreading federal aid, for GRS has rallied an impressive coalition of state and local support.

However, Congress may radically modify revenue sharing. At this writing, the states' entitlements are in serious trouble. Congressional concern over deficit spending, inflation, and the fungibility issue is a major obstacle to the renewal of GRS as a state and local revenue transfer. Moreover, the clamor on the part of the states for a balanced budget mandated by a constitutional amendment (without reducing federal grant-in-aid funding levels), growing state surpluses, and lowered state tax efforts all put the states' entitlements in jeopardy.

Finally, many of the impressive arguments in support of GRS in 1972 have been undermined by the shift in federal aid programs, specifically the movement toward consolidating narrow categorical programs into larger and more flexible block grants.

5

Block Grants: A Middle Way

A decade ago, the federal grant system could best be discussed as comprised of two types: formula-based and project-based, the latter being especially related to innovation and experimentation, and to grantsmanship. Now the system is emerging in tripartite form: categoricals, blocks, and GRS. Each of the three represents a difference on dimensions of program breadth; local discretion vs. federal decision making; targeting; and federal/local leverage in the defining of goals.

Block grants (sometimes called *blocks* or *BGs*) are the middle tier on many dimensions. It is of their essence that they, much more than the other forms of federal aid, cut across the New Federalism debates of the early seventies. They exemplify neither a continuance of the Big Brother concept of categoricals (as seen by extreme critics) nor the near-total abdication of federal responsibility for setting objectives with federal funds and for ensuring that these funds are spent in compliance with general national social policies that Nixon's special revenue sharing (SRS) concept—or at least its rhetoric—implied. Rather, as the respected ACIR states in its summary analysis of block grants as they appeared in the mid-seventies:

> The block grant, more so than other federal aid instruments, requires that a delicate balance be struck between the attainment of national goals and the exercise of recipient flexibility. Hence, it is essential that the federal agency frequently and regularly consult and communicate with states and localities on regulations and guidelines, issuances, legal rulings, policy changes, budgetary matters, reorganization, and other matters of mutual interest. . . . The federal agency has a responsibility to ensure conformance of plans and applications with statutory objectives, to evaluate recipient performance, and to keep the Congress well informed on progress in achieving national objectives. Otherwise, pressures for categorization will grow.[1]

What are these block grants? What forces brought them into being? What program areas do they cover? What impact are they having on the development of domestic policies and the delivery of needed services in our intergovernmental system? How do they differ from the categorical grants that so dominated the intergovernmental fiscal scene in the 1960s? Are they a part of the New Federalism, or a departure from the concepts underlying that phrase? These are among the questions explored in this chapter, in which we describe the major block grants now in effect.

In the previous chapter, we sketched the innovative growth of specific categoricals in the sixties and the Nixonian reaction in the early seventies. Detailed control over program decisions that needed to be made in the light of local conditions was often transferred to federal officials; "hardening of the categories" created such proliferation of minutely targeted grants that by the late sixties a local government wishing to improve its recreational amenities had to make separate applications to several different agencies if its total program included buying land for park purposes; building a swimming pool on it; operating an activity center for senior citizens; putting in trees and shrubbery; and purchasing sports equipment. In the area of urban transportation—a problem that calls for our best planning efforts in the eighties—there are separate categorical grant programs covering carpool demonstration projects; urban transportation planning; urban area traffic operations improvement; urban mass transportation basic grants (based on a formula for fund distribution); and mass transit grants (on a project application basis). Narrowness and overlapping abounded among the 492 categorical grants extant at the beginning of 1978, and this became most apparent after the explosion of such grants in a very brief (but programmatically most fecund) period, from 160 on January 1, 1963, to 379 on January 1, 1967, with 109 separate grant programs enacted in 1965 alone.[2]

As talk of a national fiscal surplus in the early sixties gave way in the early seventies to worries that the number of identified needs would far exceed public funding possibilities, economy was added to efficiency-through-consolidation as a motive for modifying the system. Finally, the ideology of localism and decentralization that characterized the Nixon administration added the spark needed to ignite a strong reaction against the perceived centralizing trend being produced by the categoricals, especially those of the project type, which gave federal officials great power through their approvals and disapprovals of grant applications from local governments. In his 1971 State of the Union message, President Nixon asserted that the national government was "so strong it becomes muscle-bound," while the states and localities "approach impotence." Decentralization of power—a "back to the people" rhetoric—was thus the activating theme behind both general revenue sharing, described in the previous chapter, and the eventual development of block grants as the residue of Nixon's companion concept, put forward (though never enacted as such) under the rubric of "special revenue sharing."

On the way to decentralization and decategorization, some intermediate steps helped to pave the way administratively for that which could only be fulfilled through legislative action. One of these was termed *Planned Variations;* another, *Annual Arrangements.* Both were experiments of the U.S. Department of Housing and Urban Development (HUD). Launched in 1971,[3] Planned Variations was designed to enlarge the authority of selected mayors to spend Model Cities program money anywhere in their cities, rather than just in the previously designated "model neighborhoods"; to waive complicating regulations of federal programs related to the Model Cities plan; and to enable mayors to review all federal spending plans for their cities—a power which the categorical grant structures were often leaving more in the hands of functional department heads than those of the generalist elected officials. Federal discretion would thus be decreased and local coordination enhanced. Some local leaders were able to make use of these powers; others were not. Annual Arrangements, inaugurated in the same year and aimed toward similar objectives, envisioned a bargaining process in which HUD administrators would get a big city's mayor to agree to adopt certain programs (such as low-income housing or affirmative action hiring), in exchange for which HUD would agree to fund a "package" of priority projects put forward by the mayor, bypassing the uncertainties of the usual multiple applications process. These administrative initiatives and the administration's community development special revenue-sharing plans both bogged down in the post-Watergate debacle, but they did help pave the way for one of the two truly major block grants of the seventies, the Community Development Block Grant program. CDBG was embedded in the Housing and Community Development (HCD) Act, which President Ford signed on August 22, 1974, as the culmination of the legislative effort begun by his predecessor in 1971.

At this point, let's quickly develop the difference between special revenue sharing (the 1971 Nixon intent) and the concept of the block grant (the 1974 reality), keeping in mind that every conceptualization is an abstraction that only approximates reality. The distinguishing marks of the SRS concept were that no application was needed and there would be no granting-agency approval required. That is, special revenue sharing would be just like its "big brother" GRS: a way of transferring funds from the national to the local level without further federal decision making, except that SRS would specify a broad area within which the recipient government must use the funds, such as community development, law enforcement, education, or manpower training. As we shall see below, where the CDBG program is analyzed in greater detail, the block grant approach allocates funds mostly by formula, greatly increases the discretion of recipient governments in making program choices, and simplifies the bureaucratic complexities through consolidation of several previously separate urban development–oriented categorical grants. However, it also requires an application and provides for disapproval by HUD unless certain fairly specific guidelines are followed, including a programmatic specification that a housing assistance plan be submitted.

At the legislative level, two block-type (though not then thought of as such) grants were enacted in the 1960s. The first of these was the Partnership for Health Act (PHA) of 1966, which consolidated 16 previously separated categorical grants (9 formula; 7 project) into a single act providing much broader functional coverage. The goal was to make federal assistance to state health agencies much more flexible, and the consolidation has indeed accomplished that with respect to the particular programs covered (including tuberculosis control, venereal disease abatement, heart disease research, and home health care). Recipient agency discretion was further enhanced by the fact that early disputes concerning the extent of federal oversight tended to be resolved in favor of the states. By the early seventies, reporting requirements had been reduced to assurances that a state plan existed to satisfy all pertinent federal requirements. But there is another side to the coin. Since passage of PHA, a number of new categorical programs have been enacted (including ones dealing with alcohol abuse, narcotic addiction, lead-based paint poisoning, urban rat control, and venereal disease) outside of the block grant structure, and the funding level of PHA now amounts to less than 4 percent of HEW's public health outlays. Comprehensive health grant appropriations peaked at $128 million in fiscal 1976 and were down to $45 million (estimated) by 1980. Thus Congress did indeed defer to state program decision making and produced a meaningful administrative simplification through consolidation of categoricals at the time PHA was passed; but it has then effectively repealed most of that accomplishment by surrounding PHA with other grants at much higher funding levels. At this time, PHA is a disappearing block grant.

The other early legislative attempt at a block grant program was the Omnibus Crime Control and Safe Streets Act of 1968. The act constitutes the only attempt so far in our grant-in-aid system to make use of the block grant type from the beginning of substantial federal involvement in a given functional area. Yet, it has been so much subjected to "creeping categorization" that it now can best be described as a closely related set of categorical grants masquerading under a block grant guise by being run through a single federal agency—the Law Enforcement Assistance Administration (LEAA)—and by utilizing state planning agency structures as a device for federal-state interaction. The major block grant segment of the Safe Streets Program covers a variety of criminal justice system elements, but Congress has greatly diminished the discretion that would otherwise be available to state and local agencies by earmarking certain percentages for correctional institutions, juvenile delinquency programs, and neighborhood crime prevention, and by requiring annual submission of comprehensive plans to LEAA for review and approval, with the specifics of this plan prescribed by law. The net result of congressional actions in the decade after enactment is well expressed in ACIR's review of block grants:

> Over the years, categorization, earmarking, and the addition of other statutory provisions have produced a complex and bewildering array of program requirements. . . . the amount of time and paperwork involved in securing most allocation changes often leaves local officials believing the block grant planning and funding allocation decisions are, at best, a ritual.[4]

ACIR has said the objective of block grants is to balance "accomplishment of national purposes within broad functional areas with the exercise of substantial recipient discretion in allocating funds to support activities which contribute to the alleviation of state and local problems."[5] If this is true, then the history of the Safe Streets Act has been one of steady movement away from the notion of substantial recipient discretion because of congressional concern, in this politically charged functional area of crime and criminal justice, that national purposes might not receive sufficient priority in each state if the degree of discretion contemplated by block grants were allowed to continue. Or, in terms of *Realpolitik*, one could say that congressmen's views of appropriate "national" purposes in this area are but a reflection of intense local pressures leading the lawmakers to wish to be on record as being in close accord with the *specific* crime concerns of their constituents.

Moving into the 1970s, we encounter President Nixon's ill-fated 1971 proposals to complement general revenue sharing with six SRS programs. These programs would have consolidated over $11-billion worth of categoricals at that time and would have covered manpower and training, law enforcement, education, transportation, urban community development, and rural community development. They would have called for no matching; would have been paid on a formula without any requirement of applications by the states or local governments; and would have had as "strings" only the requirement that the funds be spent within the six specified broad areas. Four of these have not been enacted in any form, while manpower and urban community development were passed in 1973 and 1974 as block grants.

The differences between special revenue sharing and block grants are real, but they are subtle. Perhaps we can best approach them by taking a closer look at the two major block grant programs that are in the direct lineage of the Nixon SRS proposals: the Comprehensive Employment and Training Act and the Housing and Community Development Act.

Comprehensive Employment and Training Act

The Comprehensive Employment and Training Act of 1973 (CETA) was a compromise measure that culminated four years of Nixon administration efforts to reduce the federal role in manpower to that of a funder of state and local programs as well as efforts by such interest groups as the AFL-CIO and the manpower professionals to consolidate the welter of existing categorical grants into a more manageable block while retaining significant federal authority over the programs. CETA's structure embodied carefully balanced (politically speaking) positions between categorical elements and the simpler definition of a broad functional area within which the funds were to be used, and between enhanced local discretion and national authority. As the ACIR has said, CETA was a "hybrid."

Predecessor legislation (to which CETA represents a significant but evolutionary change in federal approach) included the Manpower Development and Training Act of 1962 (MDTA), the Area Redevelopment Act of 1961, and the Economic Opportunity Act of 1964. MDTA focused on structural unemployment problems. It was designed to train the unskilled up to a minimal level of competence for the sophisticated job market of an industrialized economy and, especially, to retrain the skilled who were being displaced by the technological developments that are always changing the manpower/machinepower balance in American industry. The Area Redevelopment Act and the Economic Opportunity Act focused especially on minorities, youth, and the poverty-stricken, and they provided support services and income in addition to skills development. The acts established a new level of federal intervention in labor market affairs, far beyond the vocational education grants that had been instituted some 45 years earlier. But these programs were not considered sufficient in themselves, and by the 1970s additional categorical manpower programs—such as the Work Incentive Program, to help welfare recipients get jobs, and special training programs for blacks through the

Office of Economic Opportunity—had come into being, to the tune of 17 categoricals, making coordination a major problem. Attempts were made to reduce fragmentation of effort, and these supplied some of the ideas embodied in the legislative efforts of 1969–1973 that resulted in CETA's enactment.

What are CETA's main provisions? Title I is the true block grant segment of CETA. It provides funding by formula (unemployment rate, poverty rate, etc., in each area) for what are called *prime sponsors*, either cities or counties of 100,000 population or consortia of such general governments, in response to submission of plans which are to be prepared according to federal guidelines. For example, the plans must be directed toward the unemployed and disadvantaged in greatest need of assistance and be based upon analyses of local labor force conditions. They must also be approved by the Department of Labor (DOL)— thus maintaining real federal authority while placing the initiative for program design and priority determination in the hands of those presumably in a better position than the "federal bureaucrats" to know local needs.

Among the 17 categorical programs discontinued and folded into CETA were the Neighborhood Youth Corps, WIN, Opportunities Industrialization Centers, Vocational Rehabilitation, Work Experience and Training, and Adult Basic Education. Yet even with this consolidation, 47 other categoricals, operated through ten departments and agencies, continued to exist. (It's hard to contain any substantial function in a single government department.) The other segments of CETA are oriented toward cyclical unemployment problems (1973–1974 having begun a substantial recession that turned into stagflation and then into the 1979–1980 recession again), as Title II and Title VI (added in 1974), which fund public service jobs. They are also intended for specific clientele groups—such as Title III's manpower services earmarked for Indians, seasonal farm workers, offenders, veterans, and persons of limited English-speaking ability, and Title VIII's 1977 addition of a Young Adult Conservation Corp.

In terms of funding, the block grant portion of CETA has been increasingly dwarfed by the countercyclical elements. In fiscal 1976, Title I represented about 30 percent of the total CETA appropriation; in fiscal 1977, Title I's $1.9 billion accounted for only 15 percent of the total because Title VI had grown to 54 percent of a $12.7-billion CETA bill. And under Title VI, although the particular public service jobs to which the money is assigned are locally designated, DOL sets rather specific guidelines as to the types of positions that may be funded (e.g., specific limited projects rather than ongoing jobs, to minimize an apparent trend in some hard-pressed cities to substitute CETA money for local tax revenue in paying local civil service salaries) or the maximum salaries that may be paid. Some prime sponsors assert that the regional DOL managers apply locally irrelevant statistics in setting such rates, thus hindering local ability to fulfill the promise of the act.

The apportionment of funds among varying program elements is one rather fundamental mode of federal control in this hybrid program. How has the federal-local balance developed along other dimensions? With what success and with what problems?

It was one of the unexamined premises of the Nixon administration that a tremendous reservoir of local initiative and innovation was just waiting to be tapped, if only the federal octopus relaxed its tentacles. In fact, the first couple of years of CETA operation saw very little change from previous patterns established under the categoricals. This, we hope, was attributable in part to good targeting of the categorical programs, so that it made sense to continue what had been started. It also turned out that many local jurisdictions were seriously strained in their capabilities, half of the local governments never having run manpower programs directly before. Third, the amount of untapped imagination seems to have been overrated. While there have been some innovations (Clark County, Washington, put 25 disadvantaged youths to work doing home repair work for senior citizens; Atlanta, Georgia, developed a 24-hour skills center, with day care), the predominant note in "innovation" consisted of federal officials helping to educate local prime sponsors in the traditions of manpower expertise, through technical assistance in the writing of plans and through suggestions made in response to inadequate plans. Some localities actually complained during the first year of CETA operation that the federal government had been too passive.

Finally, local initiative's potential was blunted by ambiguities in the act itself, and in the accompanying legislative history. For example, although various community-based organizations (such as the Urban League, OIC, and other action groups that had gotten their start under OEO) were no longer directly given federal aid through project grants, the act does allude to a need for continued funding of "programs of demonstrated effectiveness." This turns out to be a euphemistic way of telling prime sponsors that they dare not ignore the groups that already have developed a local political power base in the handling of manpower programs. The most that can probably be said about the relationship of decategorization to innovation and local initiative is that *if* new ideas arise in a local context, it will be easier to incorporate them in a prime sponsor's plan and give them a try than it would have been under the pre-CETA rules.

Whatever may be the case with regard to decategorization of *program* types, it is clear that decategorization of *clientele* types reached its high point on the day that CETA was signed into law; ever since then, both administrative regulations and legislative amendments have been reparticularizing the target groups that Congress wants aided. Sometimes that will be what a local community wishes. An instance is provided in the 1978 CETA renewal, when Rep. Henry Waxman (D. Calif.) succeeded in adding senior citizens to the legislative mandate of target groups designated as "significant segments" to be aided. Congressman Waxman's district is the Fairfax area of Los Angeles, which has a large concentration of senior citizens. In this case, we have a local interest expressed at the national level by a member of Congress, with the provision added to the law then becoming a "handle" for local groups to use in pressuring their prime sponsors—an interesting triple play in the history of federalism. More often, perhaps, there is a natural tension between local and national priorities. As Mirengoff and Rindler state in a major evaluation of CETA:

There is divergence between the national emphasis upon enrolling those most in need and the tendency of local program operators to select participants likely to succeed. In the public service employment programs, national attention is riveted on creating jobs to reduce unemployment, while some local officials view the federal funds as an opportunity to support their regular local budgets or as a way to avoid higher taxes. The congressional response to situations in which there are significant local departures from national policy has been to legislate additional provisions that, in turn, limit the degree of local autonomy.[6]

Turning now to the question of decentralization of decision-making authority in CETA, what do we find? The designation of local government units as prime sponsors and the collapse of a number of categoricals into the discretionary area of the act's Title I created a milieu presumptively conducive to a major shift of program decisions from federal officials to the "locals" who would be in close touch with their situations in their own labor markets. In the long history of intergovernmental funding, however, opportunities for local units to spend funds supplied by the national government have also created temptations to siphon such funding into areas of local priority. CETA proved to be no exception. The act emphasized needs of the disadvantaged, but local use often "creamed" the clientele pool: Those selected for participation were often those for whom job placement was thought to be easiest rather than those most in need of having their skills upgraded. CETA's goal was to train and place, and it was assumed that each year a new group of clients would be served. But prime sponsors (keep in mind that these are city and county officials) in a number of jurisdictions began using CETA's public service employment provisions as a way of funding regular civil service positions indefinitely. Political patronage and nepotism cropped up in a number of cities in a manner reminiscent of the WPA programs of the Great Depression.

The congressional response to publicized instances of abuse and evidence of unanticipated forms of local "imagination" in using CETA's funds has been—as is generally the case with grant programs as the government moves from enactment through a few years of implementation—to enact restrictive conditions and to establish monitoring and auditing systems that re-create much of the paperwork that decentralization was supposed to have eliminated. And as Congress and the Department of labor make almost annual changes in their requirements and guidelines, local governments complain again about federal interference. In this connection, it's interesting to read a comment made in 1978 by Moon Landrieu, who had been mayor of New Orleans and who in 1979 became Secretary of Housing and Urban Development in the Carter cabinet: "CETA would have done better locally if the feds would quit changing the rules, quit changing the philosophy, quit changing the guidelines, and give the program a chance."

Given the political fact that CETA emerged as a compromise between those who felt the objective was to shift power back to the local level and those who wished to assure that federal dollars were spent to enhance federally defined objectives, it is not surprising that Mirengoff and Rindler characterize the legislative history as leaving "a large gray area in which the reach of the local authorities contends with the grasp of the federal establishment."[7] That gray area was tipped toward national authority almost from the beginning through planning requirements that called for prime sponsors to submit to DOL an annual CETA plan that included an analysis of manpower problems in the area; identification of populations needing assistance; a description of program activities to be undertaken; service delivery plans; and a statement of expected results.[8]

By 1977, program evaluation monitoring by DOL had progressed to the stage of quantitative measures of placements, cost ratios per client served, etc. There was strong local opposition to DOL's performance guidelines, and new compromises had to be developed. Mirengoff and Rindler write of "gradual erosion" of local flexibility and state that the stream of directives had by 1978 become a "torrent." The final months of 1978 also saw a proliferating number of newspaper and magazine stories about political and fiscal abuses in the program, making it clear that the balance of decentralization is not easily struck. A major issue is: Can management and substance be separated in such a way that the national government assures itself of proper administration of the act while leaving to local prime sponsors the decisions about who to serve through which delivery agencies and programs? Our view is that the national government's role is properly more than that of an auditor, that without substituting its judgment of local conditions for that of the prime sponsors, it should, as Mirengoff and Rindler recommend, "interpret national policies and issue annual statements of priorities for prime sponsor guidance," thus providing a national perspective within which local implementation decisions can be made.[9]

For example, the President's 1975 *Manpower Report* questioned the degree to which countercyclical goals (quickly creating public project jobs in times of rising unemployment) were compatible with human resource development goals, which call for sustained training, skill upgrading, and supportive service efforts. To the extent that these cannot be maximized simultaneously within a given budget of time and money, the issue calls for a national determination of priorities, though local choice may then appropriately assess the precise actions to be taken for a given year. Annual policy-and-priority statements, carefully written after discussions between DOL staff and the program's overseeing congressional subcommittees, might with luck go some distance toward alleviating the legislators' felt need to recategorize and recentralize. Without such a development, we may well lose the real gains that CETA represents by providing some elbow room in which local governments can adapt national program objectives and resources to specific local conditions.

Housing and Community Development Act

One of the most interesting and largest block grants of the New Federalism era is the Housing and Community Development Act of 1974. It is more often referred to as the Community Development Block Grant Program (CDBG) because Titles I and II authorize federal assistance for community development and housing assistance for low- and moderate-income groups. The 1974 act and the 1977 renewal legislation authorized over $18 billion through 1980, divided between eligible and discretionary jurisdictions by a formula discussed below.

CDBG—THE MECHANICAL ISSUES

It is important to note that the CDBG approach is quite different from that of previous housing and community development programs. Before the 1974 act, most housing and community development programs were enacted by a single piece of legislation, but implemented separately. For example, urban renewal legislation would enact a series of housing, slum clearance, and rehabilitation programs under the umbrella of one legislative act. However, each of these programs would be implemented independently, giving rise to duplication, red tape, and programs working at cross-purposes. Jurisdictions willing to engage in community development activities usually had to apply for each program separately and didn't have much discretion in putting together their own mix of programs.

The Housing and Community Development Act changed all this. It consolidated the following seven categorical grants into one block grant authorization:

1. rehabilitation loans;
2. urban renewal/neighborhood development programs;

3. Model Cities;
4. neighborhood facilities programs;
5. open space programs;
6. public facilities loans;
7. water and sewer facilities programs.

Eligible jurisdictions are now free to package their own plans out of this array.

In keeping with the philosophical tenets of the New Federalism, CDBG is not allocated on a competitive basis. Rather, the CDBG program provides for an automatic grant to cities of at least 50,000 and to urban counties on a needs formula. Nonmetropolitan governments and jurisdictions not automatically entitled to funding can compete for roughly 20 percent of CDBG that is earmarked for discretionary awards.

Administered by HUD, CDBG is an attempt to increase the policy-making power of local general-purpose governments. Unlike GRS, however, CDBG does not come relatively string-free. There are "national objectives" in the HCD Act of 1974, and a series of application procedures and requirements must be met *before* a recipient jurisdiction receives its entitlement.

Congress mandated seven national objectives that HUD is to use as yardsticks in approving applications. The most important (and controversial) is the requirement that CDBG monies be used for "the elimination of slums and blight and the prevention of blighting influences and the deterioration of property and neighborhood and community facilities of importance to the welfare of the community, principally persons of low and moderate income." Even though a jurisdiction may be automatically eligible, it must develop its priorities with an eye toward these goals. To ensure that national objectives are achieved, each jurisdiction must submit, as part of its application, a three-year community development plan, a one-year priority program, and a housing assistance plan (HAP).

Moreover, each jurisdiction must certify that in developing these plans, "maximum feasible priority" was given to projects that will benefit low- and moderate-income families. Each jurisdiction must also demonstrate that adequate citizen participation was solicited in the formulating of the three- and one-year plans. There are also civil rights provisions, Davis-Bacon requirements, environmental impact statements, and the need to route an application through the A-95 process.

An examination of these binding requirements demonstrates the differences between GRS and the CDBG program. CDBG does allow considerably more local discretion and planning than the categorical grants it incorporated in that recipient jurisdictions put together their *own* community development strategies and priorities. HUD's role is to screen out applications that "clearly" are at odds with the authorizing legislation's national goals. Consequently, national objectives and federal guidance are part of the application (and evaluation) process—yet local direction and goal setting are encouraged.

THE EARLY FINDINGS

The monitoring studies of the Brookings Institution spotlight the difficulties of trying simultaneously to decentralize federal community development programs and to achieve national goals.[10]

CDBG, as opposed to GRS, was thought of as old money in a new form. The early monitoring studies focusing on the first two rounds thus show a use pattern that does not reliably indicate future developments. A number of jurisdictions were committed to funding the consolidated categoricals that compose CDBG, and so they continued to fund such projects out of their CDBG entitlements. However, it is interesting to review briefly the findings of the Brookings Institution studies to provide background information on the 1977 amendments that, as we shall see, strengthened the federal government's monitoring role.

The first year's data show a twofold use pattern: (1) continuing support (sometimes at a lower level) for the collapsed categoricals; and (2) a new emphasis on housing rehabilitation, public improvements, etc. The emphasis on capital expenditures was at the expense of continuing support for the old categoricals. That is to say, the most distressed neighborhoods received less support under CDBG than under the separate categorical programs that CDBG superseded.

The Brookings study also noted that "the CDBG program did not significantly contribute to the legislative objective of encouraging 'spatial deconcentration' of housing for lower-income persons."[11] Moreover, capital spending (50 percent at times) was allocated for short-term projects. It can be argued that a few houses rehabilitated here and there do not add up to a comprehensive community development plan.

Again, to quote the Brookings study: "These first-year findings suggest that the block grant program is a better instrument for aiding transitional neighborhoods and preventing blight than were the folded-in grants, but that it is more limited as an instrument for redeveloping the most seriously deteriorated urban areas."[12] By shifting resources under the CDBG to neighborhoods not as fiscally depressed or blighted as others, CDBG might postpone indefinitely the redevelopment of the most severely affected areas of the country. It was not accidental that Congress tightened the strings when the HCD Act came up for renewal.

143

THE 1977 AMENDMENTS

The 1977 renewal legislation and HUD's revised regulations expanded the scope of federal intrusion into the planning and implementation state of CDBG at the local level.

First, a congressional compromise developed a dual formula to improve the targeting of CDBG funds to hard-pressed jurisdictions. The 1974 law had a "phase out" requirement that would have drastically cut the funds available for older urban jurisdictions. The 1977 dual formula approach assures the north central and eastern regions, especially, that their funding will not be less than the total dollar amount they received under the now collapsed categoricals for community development. This reverses, at least in small part, the spreading effect inherent in New Federalism programs at the expense of regions and jurisdictions fiscally in need.

HUD also became involved in the targeting issue. New regulations restricted the amount that could be allocated for neighborhoods *not* falling under the low- and moderate-income test. HUD became increasingly involved in the application stage, engaging in "intergovernmental diplomacy" when a jurisdiction's application was not acceptable. Citizen participation issues were also refined; no longer would certification of participation at a community-wide level be acceptable. On March 1, 1978, HUD required a two-tier approach that introduced neighborhood as well as community-wide participation. Low-income groups now have a better chance of influencing projects.

The tightening of the formula for improving the targeting of CDBG funds and HUD's more assertive role are counterbalances made necessary by a critical flaw in the philosophy behind New Federalism programs: The assumption that decentralization will lead to the achievement of national goals without strong federal supervision. Let's quickly review a number of problems with CDBG to substantiate this argument.

CDBG: AN ASSESSMENT

CDBG, much like GRS, spreads scarce resources too thinly. While it is true that almost every jurisdiction in the country has a need (of one type or another) for federal assistance, it is not true that each jurisdiction has an equal need. CDBG operations cannot be monitored by HUD in ways that ensure compliance with the legislatively mandated objectives. Decentralization has simplified application forms and requirements. Consequently, HUD's information base is limited. A report by the U.S. General Accounting Office noted that

> HUD does not obtain from recipient communities the information needed to evaluate community performance and to assure itself and the Congress that CDBG programs are developed in accordance with the legislative objectives of (1) benefiting low- and moderate-income persons, (2) aiding in preventing or eliminating slums or blight, or (3) meeting other community development needs having a particular urgency.[13]

It would seem that simplification may also reduce government's role in addressing national problems.

This "hands off" approach on the part of HUD has far-reaching consequences for the local political process. While HUD changed its original position on participation, it did not go one step further and specify the form (as opposed to level) of participation required in developing CDBG applications. Each jurisdiction is free to develop its own form (e.g., citizen advisory groups) of participation. However, what works well in, say, New York City will not work at all in Little Rock, Arkansas, without federal monitoring and prescribed standards. We believe HUD should require two

145

or three successful forms for local jurisdictions to choose from, rather than leave this open-ended. In many cases, low-income groups can be systematically excluded from participating if the form of participation is structured to achieve a predetermined outcome.

A final objection can be raised against CDBG and the New Federalism in general: The objectives in the authorizing legislation are not specific enough. The best one can "hold on to" are a long laundry list of expectations and activities that qualify for funding. However, fragmented activities, no matter how noble, do not add up to a comprehensive community development strategy. Still, given the above problems, the CDBG experience can be praised on several counts.

CDBG: A POSITIVE NOTE

First of all, CDBG is a major step toward recognizing the diversity of subnational problems and solutions. Local participants form a better partnership with the federal government in trying to address common problems. For example, the 1977 amendments allow for greater private sector involvement in CDBG activities. The types of activities and private sector contracts are to be worked out at the local level, thus reducing the burden of performance monitoring on the part of the federal government and shifting this burden to the recipient jurisdiction, which should know its own needs and resources best.

CDBG is a mechanism that could (with a number of changes) provide recipient jurisdictions with the resources to plan comprehensively; certainly the flexibility is there. If changes in the participation requirement were made (e.g., mandated forms and closer monitoring by HUD), CDBG might stimulate citizen participation in projects in their own neighborhoods.

Title XX—Social Services

There is one more quasi–block grant program that deserves
brief mention: The state social service program provisions
enacted by Congress in 1974 and generally referred to as
the Title XX Program. This one has a curious history, illus-
trative of the trial-and-error process by which we often
develop public policy in the United States.

In 1967, Congress enacted amendments to the Social Security Act to help the states fund programs designed to help
people get off the so-called welfare rolls, as well as to make
available services that mere money to individuals would not
take care of, such as temporary facilities for abused children.
This was an open-ended grant-in-aid program in which the
federal government paid to any state $3 for every dollar the
state spent on social service programs. Because three fourths
of the money would come from the federal government and
the funding was open-ended, the states had an incentive to
increase their programs without worrying too much about
costs; and by the beginning of the 1970s, the aggregate bill
being presented to the federal government was beginning to
skyrocket. Also, in many instances the states seem not to
have been restricting their social service programs to the
poor and near-poor, as was the congressional intent. In
1972, Congress therefore imposed a $2.5-billion annual ceiling
on Title XX payments, and HEW set about developing
guidelines for the kinds of programs on which federal dollars
could be spent, in areas ranging from day care to job coun-
seling.

Congress became unhappy with the draft HEW regulations and at the end of 1974 passed legislation (PL93–647)
that spelled out some specific guidelines for the operation
of this program. Among other things, Congress required the

states to use at least 50 percent of their payments to provide services to welfare recipients; offer at least three kinds of services to the aged poor; offer family planning services to families receiving aid to families with dependent children payments; provide at least one service program oriented toward each of five specified program goals (such as economic self-support or prevention of inappropriate institutional care through community-based programs); and maintain their program efforts at existing levels. (The last provision was designed to prevent the substitution of federal for state dollars, thus freeing state dollars for other purposes without accomplishing more within the social service areas.)

One can quickly see that this set of regulations does not exactly leave the states free to do whatever they want. At the same time, substantial discretion remains in state hands, as compared with the operation of a project approval system. States must submit social service program plans to HEW as well as end of year reports on the actual use of federal social service payments. Yet, Title XX is on a formula basis within the legislated program areas and thus shares in the general concept of block grants as a middle ground between the revenue sharing and categorical grant approaches.

The Block Grant Experience Revised

The accelerated movement toward greater use of the block grant format has highlighted the "myth of decentralization"— the belief that national goals can be achieved by decentralizing subnational choice and policy priorities within broad federal parameters. Once this bubble is burst, corollary questions arise: Is decentralization needed in all functional areas? Do all recipient jurisdictions have the administrative infrastructure to implement their own programs if Washington picks up the bill?

It can be argued, based on the experience of the last two decades, that the answer on both counts is "No!"

In many instances, block grants push counties, small towns, and cities into activities that they are neither prepared for nor want to become involved in. To develop manpower (CETA), housing (CDBG), and transportation programs requires a high level of political support, technical sophistication, and bureaucratic expertise. Clearly not all of the eligible jurisdictions for block grant funding come close to these minimum requirements.

Consequently, when these jurisdictions fail to meet federal expectations, a case of "administrative creep" develops. In the case of CETA, guidelines were tightened; for CDBG, the rules of the game were changed to ensure that low-income populations would be the chief beneficiaries. In both cases, subnational officials felt betrayed and frustrated, and the stereotypical pictures that federal and local actors have of each other (see chapter 4) were reinforced.

From the federal perspective, however, changing the rules was the only way to ensure compliance with national objectives. If cooperation is to be the hallmark of intergovernmental relations in the 1980s, then the block grant experience of the 1970s can be viewed as at least partially counterproductive.

The myth of decentralization also assumes that the states will provide the needed support mechanisms for "first time" jurisdictions to engage in complex substate problem solving. However, two of the most important block grant programs, for the most part, bypass state capitals. CDBG and CETA are direct federal-substate programs. Moreover, GRS allocates two thirds of the pot to local jurisdictions. Given the recent pandering to states-rights' arguments, the block grant experience is a continuing way to undermine state autonomy.

The federal government, recognizing this major flaw in the

block grant approach, has tried to develop incentives to entice state governments into assuming a more influential role. As a 1979 ACIR publication points out:

> The recent state interest in the development of community assistance strategies derives at least in part from federal encouragement. The strongest of the federal influences appears to have been the January, 1978, White House Conference on Planned National Growth and Economic Development, which sought actively to direct state attentions toward local development needs.
>   . . . A second federal influence was the Carter Urban Policy released in March, 1978, which formally recognized the states as partners in the development of a national community conservation strategy.[14]

The block grant experience has stimulated greater federal-state cooperation in theory, but the true impact has yet to be assessed.

We must address a series of questions before we can evaluate the decentralized block grant alternative:

1. To what extent can local generalists successfully implement complex federal programs?
2. How can the spreading effect of the New Federalism target scarce resources?
3. Given the methodological problems, how can the federal government monitor subnational compliance with national goals?
4. What is the policy and programmatic relationship between GRS, CDBG, CETA, and other block grants?

The New Federalism and the myth of decentralization have a long way to go before such questions are satisfactorily answered.

Now let's turn to a review of the pros and cons of block grants and an overall evaluation.

Why have so few block grants been enacted, despite rather widespread agreement that the categorical system has become rigid, overly detailed, and administratively very cumbersome? What does it take to consolidate a lot of related specific programs into a block grant? A major key is provided in what ACIR lists as one of seven conditions under which it recommends use of blocks: that a "high degree of consensus over general purposes exists among the Congress, the federal administering agency, and recipients."[15] General consensus often does *not* exist among competing defenders of specific programs. Each fears that even if the total of federal aid after consolidation were to be the same as before, its pet program might not be the preferred one among aid-receiving state and local units. Each group would have to fight its battles in many jurisdictions rather than just on Capitol Hill if the states had increased discretion within a block allocation that replaced several previously mandated special programs.

Nor would opposition to block consolidation be limited to the interested groups that had earlier fought long and hard to accomplish a specific legislative goal, now seen as potentially to be swallowed up. Congressional views, reflecting diverse constituencies, are not often in synchronization with the views of the functional specialist—the technocrats— of the administering agencies. Value judgments about the "worthiness" of ultimate beneficiary groups differ sharply, as do perceptions of factual conditions and causal linkages in regard to social conditions—which perceptions in turn of course affect one's sense of rational priorities. Only occasionally will some general consideration of political structure —such as the Nixon administration's preoccupation with minimizing the federal role—take precedence over program politics in determining a legislative outcome. Administrative principles can rarely be made to appear as "sexy" as program needs. One such occasion was in 1968, when the politically sensitive tradition of state-local control over police forces made decentralization a major consideration in the design of the Safe Streets Act.

Despite the obstacles, the block grant device has some distinct advantages. From the national legislative perspective, it's a good political compromise. The congressman or senator can help shape a national program in an area of constituent interest and can establish administrative machinery for a postaudit type of fiscal and programmatic accountability. At the same time, he/she lets state and local elected officials take credit for detailed program decisions that accommodate to local priorities—or blame for unpopular choices. From a state-local perspective, BGs mean a lessening of paperwork (and that's no small accomplishment in any administrative organization today!) and a shifting of decisional power from functional specialists to the generalists—which at least should tend to accord more with notions of democratic accountability. Finally, block grants have the potential to draw together related programs into wholes that may be much more than the sums of their parts. When local directors of programs previously funded independently all receive their resources from a single point and have their activities planned and reported jointly, there is a strong incentive for more effective program cooperation and integration. From the viewpoint of the clientele groups to which programs of social services, recreation, education, or health are directed, such integration is extremely important in terms of frustration-avoidance as well as of program effectiveness in a direct sense.

What are the central problems affecting BGs' prospects? The major problem affecting existing block grants is, clearly, "creeping categorization"; that is, the strong tendency in both Congress and the executive branch to nibble away at the broad grants of discretion given to state-local governments in the block grants. Part of this is administrative defensiveness, in anticipation of congressional ire if scandals in fund use should become significant—as was the case with CETA in 1977–1979. If more monitoring is done by the federal administering agency, and more approvals are required, then fewer opportunities for mistakes and malfeasance will exist. The outstanding example of creeping categorization is not CETA but the Omnibus Crime Control Act. A chart issued by the LEAA units and program segments graphically illustrates how an originally rather simple, broad block structure can change, by program accretions and subcategorizations, into a structure that may better be described as an aggregation of categoricals. LEAA used 15 boxes in its diagram of the 1968 structure but 61 in its diagram of the maze that had developed by 1976.[16]

For both existing and prospective block grants, a second truly major problem, conceptually and socio-scientifically as well as politically, is that of developing meaningful indexes by which to target federal aid so that taxpayers' dollars can be best spent. Let us take countercyclical public jobs programs as an example. Conceptually, the measurement of need should include those known as "discouraged workers" (those who want a job, but who have given up looking), but how do you estimate the size of this group? Or should public policy cease to worry about them on the grounds that they are "undeserving" because lacking in initiative? In terms of community development, are "needs" for such amenities as municipal tree trimming and the provision of sidewalks and curbs in middle-class areas less important than housing and children's playgrounds in "blighted" urban neighborhoods? As we have seen in the case of both GRS and CDBG, such questions are not easy to answer, and all formulas turn

out to have unforeseeable, or at least unforeseen, consequences. In the formula–block grant world, knowledge of
how to use the United States Census becomes an essential
matter for both social science technicians in federal agencies
and for legislators who wish to see computer printouts of
how their constituents would fare under alternative funding
provisions. The targeting concept's programmatic rationality
contests perpetually with the political logic of spreading the
gravy into the maximum number of legislative districts—a
necessary condition, often, in building a majority coalition
for a new program.

In short, block grants are conceptually "neat" and have
some political and programmatic advantages. They are unlikely, however, to become more than a modifying influence
upon the overwhelmingly categorically oriented thrust of
the intergovernmental grant system. In fiscal 1975, the major
block grant group (CETA, CDBG, Partnership in Health,
and Title XX social services) accounted for 8.4 percent of
federal aid; for fiscal 1980 the advance estimate was 10.6 percent—but at the expense of general revenue sharing, which
was expected to fall from 12.7 percent share in 1975 to 8.6
percent in 1980, rather than of categoricals, which were
scheduled to go from 78.9 percent in the earlier year to 80.8
percent in 1980. Categoricals continue to dominate the intergovernmental fiscal landscape, and we expect that they will
do so in the future. Fragmented, interest-group politics
necessarily produce fragmented, particularistic programs.

III

Prognosis and Prescription

6

In Praise of Permissive Federalism

It is time to ask ourselves: What have we established through our review of fiscal federalism, the grant-in-aid system, revenue sharing, and block grants? If one had to make a single statement in reply, it might be that federal financial aid has created a nationally dominated system of shared power and shared functions. General revenue sharing has not become a sufficiently substantial factor to affect this judgment. More extensive movement toward GRS could shift the pattern toward a state-dominated system of shared functions, but such movement is most unlikely. In either case, it is clear that the basic relationship between the nation and the states today, whatever the theory or practice of federalism may have been earlier, is one of interdependence rather than independence. Furthermore, the interdependence involves mutual leverage insofar as power relations are concerned: Although the national government is basically dominant, the states and localities retain sufficient political strength to ensure that their views will be listened to by the national government in designing its programs, and that they will have considerable discretion in the implementation of federally funded programs.

Now let's look at these elements in greater detail. First of all, why do we say that the system is nationally dominated? When we look at the power of state and local governments to resist, and at the choices of project grants available to them, it might seem that they rather than Uncle Sam are in the driver's seat. However, the picture changes sharply if we compare the present system with that which would obtain if GRS were the general pattern. In comparative terms, there can be no doubt: Categorical grants and block grants comprise a system in which the fundamental program choices in the expenditure of federal funds are made on the basis of national priorities.

Another comparison is also relevant. If we compare the reach of the federal government today with that which existed prior to World War II, we would have to say that the range of public sector decisions subject to national government influence is immeasurably greater now. This is partly a matter of general policy requirements attached to grants and partly a matter of the tone that the federal government sets even in unaided functional areas. If merit criteria are enforced in grant employment, by requirement, there's a strong push to eliminate the spoils system in non-grant employment in the same jurisdiction. Civil rights legislation operates both as direct federal law and as a "string" attached to all grants and contracts which require affirmative action employment efforts throughout the jurisdiction of the receiving agency.

When we speak of a nationally dominated governmental system, we do not mean that the national government makes all the decisions so much as that it now greatly affects many decisions it does not make. This spillover effect could hardly operate as a strong factor unless something else of a quite intangible nature had taken place; namely, a much broader acceptance of the national government's legitimacy than was the norm when the states'-rights conception of federalism held sway over most of the nation. Acceptance of national government priorities in grant-in-aid programs is only one manifestation of this enhanced legitimacy of Washington in domestic affairs. As suggested earlier in this book, both court decisions and nonfinancial legislation in areas of civil rights, pesticide regulation, occupational health standards, and the establishment of air and water antipollution requirements are now largely taken for granted, but less than a generation ago these would have been considered severe violations of the vulgarized Tenth Amendment form of federalism.

The vote for 18-year-olds is a good illustration of the sea change that has occurred in our expectations regarding federalism. When Congress passed legislation giving 18-year-olds the right to vote in national elections, there was some question as to whether the Supreme Court would uphold this assertion of national authority. It did, and without any general outcry. That was quickly followed by the ratification of a constitutional amendment extending the 18-year-old vote to all elections. Thus does another previously exclusive area of state jurisdiction—control over elections—topple before the notion that the United States constitutes a single national community. Federally imposed limits placed in 1979 on thermostat settings in public buildings are yet another example of the national government's accepted reach.

But political life is complex. Having established that our overall system is now nationally dominated in the senses indicated, we must point out that the dominance is often greater in potential than in actuality, and that it coexists with a great deal of operational autonomy on the part of the states and localities—even with victories by the lower jurisdictions in specific instances. The dependence of national political authority upon a heavily decentralized party system, as Grodzins has stressed, has a good deal to do with this mutuality of leverage. For example, when the U.S. Department of Health, Education and Welfare attempted in 1965 to withhold funds from the city of Chicago because of questions about that city's compliance with federal requirements, the political clout of Mayor Daley within the Democratic party brought a quick resumption of funding. Even aside from the party system's influence, however, state and local governments would have substantial power in the discretionary implementation of federally aided programs simply because of the fact of interdependence and the one practical administrative consequence of formal federalism—the inability of federal officials to fire recalcitrant state or local government employees.

Where conflicting interests and values are at stake—as they always are in public policy—few questions are settled "on the merits" since the merits themselves are part of what is in question. Power and influence depend on persuasion, it's true, but persuasiveness is considerably enhanced when the persuader has some sanctions over the one he/she is attempting to persuade. Anyone who has authority to fire us can count on our listening attentively to his/her thoughts and preferences. Since this kind of authority relationship over personnel within an organization is the ultimate sanction underlying all lesser sanctions, its absence from the relationship between federal grantors and state-local grantees considerably dilutes the reach of the former. Even within a single organization where this sanction does exist, we have learned through the theory of informal organization—especially from the seminal writings of Chester I. Barnard— that authority is much more elusive than the simplistic notion of one person being in a position to give orders to another.[1] An executive has authority over his/her employees to the extent that they accept his/her right to direct their behavior, that is, to the extent that they consider his/her claim to authority to be "legitimate." This assessment in turn may rest upon another perception: Whether the executive can claim their allegiance on the basis of superior expertise, superior knowledge of the situation, or simply legal power. If authority in an organization that does possess hiring and firing powers nevertheless rests upon the consent of the governed, then all the more so does the achievement of federal purposes in the aided programs depend upon the willing cooperation of the grantee governments. And they are unlikely to concede even a theoretical legitimacy of superior knowledge, since they will see themselves as having a monopoly on knowledge of the particular local situation.

Yet another qualification demonstrates the futility of attempting generalized answers to questions about the distribution of national power: What we have been saying about state-local leverage applies mostly to formula grants and much less so to project grants. In formula grants, the burden of proof is on the national government to show that there is good reason to withhold what the law automatically grants on the basis of certain minimal general conditions. (This applies also to CETA and CDBG, as block grants are akin to formula categoricals in this respect.) When a project grant is at stake, however, the burden of proof shifts to the proposing state or local agency, for it must show that it warrants the grant requested on the basis of a proposal superior to those of competing applicants. Or, we can say that formula grants are given "of right" while project grants represent "a privilege." At the more general level of state-local participation in the development of the outlines of national programs—specifically including state-local influence in seeing that new national programs are developed within the grant-in-aid context rather than becoming direct operations of the central government—we would expect that source of influence to remain as vigorous as ever for the foreseeable future. Whether loosely structured, undisciplined, locally oriented political parties are cause or consequence of constitutional formalities of federalism (and whichever came first, the relationship appears to be one of symbiosis now), the effect of both is to give a much more localized tone to so-called national programs than would otherwise be the case. Grodzins states the matter well:

> The political potency of the local organization has a very important effect on national policy. In at least one sense, it makes a counterweight against the tendency to centralize power in Washington. The history of legislation with respect to many important programs . . . shows national legislators writing national legislation with a sensitive ear to state and local political leaders. This is a natural tendency in the light of political realities: The American national legislator considers himself the representative of district and state interests because his position is secured through the efforts of state and district—not national—political organizations.
>
> The politics of administration is a process of making peace with legislators who for the most part consider themselves the guardians of local interests. The political role of administrators therefore contributes to the power of states and localities in national programs.[2]

In addition to all of the factors above that qualify national dominance, there is another that operates even in the absence of state-local demands. It is buck passing by the national government. The reader may recall that Philip Monypenny explains the whole grant-in-aid system as a compromise based on the fact that interest groups wanting certain government actions are sometimes strong enough to move Congress in the desired direction while not unified sufficiently to demand an integrated, directly national program. The other side of this coin is that the national legislature, in the words of Martha Derthick, uses the grant system

> to commit itself to serving very broad national purposes (such as "more adequate" welfare) without assuming the burden of making all of the political choices it would have to make in a unitary system (how much welfare, for whom?). The difficult choices may be left to other governments.[3]

She adds that the vitality of the American Congress in comparison with the legislatures of other nations "may be attributed partly to the opportunities the federal system provides for responding to pressures for action while limiting the risks of the response."[4]

It has long been noted in the literature on government regulation of business that the independent regulatory commissions (such as the Federal Communications Commission, Interstate Commerce Commission, and Federal Power Commission) operate at a considerable political disadvantage vis-à-vis the interests they are supposed to regulate because the statutes empowering them are so vague regarding the goals and standards that they are to enforce. For example, the FCC is required to allocate radio and television frequencies on the basis of "the public interest, necessity, and convenience"—whatever this may mean. This is legislative buck passing, because Congress is not simply being reticent; rather, it is reflecting its own lack of consensus. It knows only that it wants to regulate but cannot agree on how much regulation. It therefore gives a blank check of undetermined value, as it were, to the administrative agency. In similar fashion, much grant-in-aid legislation reflects the presence of a congressional consensus that action should be taken in a particular sphere, and eqaully the absence of a congressional consensus regarding exactly what that action should be, or how much action. Again, as Derthick points out, to formulate precise and internally consistent policies is always difficult, but "grant programs may magnify the difficulties because the extremely diverse interests of all state governments are directly engaged in the programs' operation."[5]

The rise of block grant programs carries the buck-passing syndrome further. While Washington retains some ultimate leverage with which to nudge state-local governments toward national priorities, the program design responsibility is placed on the subnational units, and it is they who must work out the political compromises among competing clientele groups. The federal role then becomes the less risky one (as compared with a project system) of ratifying what the local political authorities have worked out.

What Are the Trends?

We have just sketched the situation as of today. Now it is time to ask: What are the predictable trends in the future evolution of the system? First, it seems safe to say that the states and localities will become even more dependent upon federal financial assistance in the next few years. The service demands that a growing population and urban complexity make upon these governments cannot but increase, and more than proportionately to the rate of population growth. Public sector services constitute a major and increasing portion of the American standard of living, and as Gross National Product rises, so do our expectations for public services, especially those that are needed for the full enjoyment of related private expenditures. Proposition 13 sentiment may slow these trends but will not reverse them.

164

IN PRAISE OF PERMISSIVE FEDERALISM

For example, the more we spend on putting a second car in each suburban garage, the more we need to spend on highways, traffic signals, policemen, and traffic court judges. The more money we have in our pockets privately, the more we go on vacation, and when we go on vacation we make ever greater use of public facilities. Visitors to the national park system increased from approximately 130 million in 1969 to 170 million in 1970 and topped 200 million in 1971. To camp overnight in one of California's state beach parks on the Pacific Ocean, one must make a reservation for July or August in January or February. If gasoline shortages force more local vacations, urban park and recreation facilities will require greater expansion.

To the assertion that the federal financial role in the intergovernmental system will increase further, there are two qualifications to be made. First, part of that increase may take the indirect form of federal tax credits for state income taxes. We say this because it seems clear that the debate over revenue sharing has brought the inadequacies of state-local tax effort into public view to such an extent that reform must result. Almost all intergovernmental fiscal experts believe the states could considerably increase their own revenues if they all adopted income taxes and extended these taxes to higher progressive rates—perhaps even making all state income taxes a percentage of federal income taxes paid. This won't happen without federal prodding, however. To the extent that the federal government succeeds with the carrot of tax credits, it is of course subsidizing the state tax deductions already embedded in the federal income tax system. That subsidy will not show up on the figures on grants-in-aid. A second way in which the domestic role of the national government will increase without affecting fiscal federal statistics lies in the assumption by the national government of services previously handled on a shared basis or not included in the public sector at all. We refer here, of course, to the assumption of welfare costs by Washington, but also to the very clearly predictable extension of at least a portion of public medical care financing from the aged to the entire population.

Because of both ideology and a political structure that often enables interest groups to obtain program authorization at the national level while leaving the hard decisions about exact content to the state level, however, domestic public services will continue to be handled on a shared basis, both fiscally and operationally. If there ever was a time of separated functions (and we believe there once was to a considerable extent, despite the Grodzins-Elazar contentions to the contrary), as the dual federalism proponents have always assumed, then those days are gone forever. In the future, functions will be separated by level of government only when the federal government, to ensure even-handed administration, entirely takes over certain services previously performed on a shared basis. And that's not exactly what the voices crying in the wilderness for a revised states'-rights federalism have in mind.

A third prediction—one we think is a very safe bet—is that the predominant mode of federal financial assistance will continue to be that of categorical grants, with some attempts at consolidation looking toward block grants. Revenue sharing, in the true sense of funds supplied without programmatic strings of any kind, is not likely to increase its share of the grant-in-aid pie.

We may indeed end up with some old wine in apparently new bottles, and although a little bit confusing, this will not really change the situation. As we have seen, block grant programs enacted in lieu of special revenue sharing tend toward recategorization rather soon after enactment. On this point there cannot be any doubt. Every time Congress begins with a broad grant of authority, it ends up changing that broad grant into a series of specific grants as it receives feedback information on uses of the funds that it finds are politically popular and those that cause political trouble. And after all, isn't this programmatically as well as politically sensible?

At the beginning, the legislators may want sufficient experimentation to find out what approach to a problem works best. Once one receives results from a number of localities— using the states as experimental laboratories but with federal funds—then would it not be foolish to continue the unfettered freedom rather than to require that the method proven most successful be adopted by all jurisdictions?

Finally, we expect a continued development of the notion of a national community and continued acceptance of the corollary proposition that it is proper for the goals and standards of public services to be set by the national government as a basis for uniform rights of citizens—no matter where they live. Perhaps it was once thought appropriate to accept differentials in services between states on the basis that a person was a citizen of one state or another, and it was up to each state to determine what level of services it wanted to provide. Under that conception, we cannot complain if we live in Arkansas or Vermont and our children receive less than minimal per pupil expenditures, while those who happen to reside in California or Massachusetts or New York enjoy superior education simply by being citizens of another state.

Increasingly, we are arguing, Americans are coming to define certain basic services as "rights" of *national* citizenship, and among these services are education, medical care, and public assistance for the poor. The civil rights movement and the Supreme Court's response to it in the form of fleshing out the Fourteenth Amendment may have performed a great service for all citizens by compelling us to confront the value choices inherent in the distinction between asserting the primacy of state citizenship and that of national citizenship. Equality before the law, as guaranteed by the Fourteenth Amendment, is confined in the terms of that amendment to certain specific kinds of discrimination; but by analogy it is being extended broadly to equality of social services regardless of geographic location within the country. Combined with the general cultural homogenization created by the media and the ease of transportation, this trend means the end of much of the social diversity that is the only logical basis for continuation of old-style federalism in the sense of acceding to the different value norms of different geographic areas.

What Does Federalism Mean Now?

The Constitution has been properly described as a living document, one whose provisions must be reinterpreted in each age lest there develop an unbridgeable "generation gap" between the founding fathers and the electorate of the present day. Because we accept substantive changes more easily when they can be covered by the old labels—thus permitting us to fool ourselves into thinking that change is less than it really is—we are likely to go on using the word *federalism* with content greatly changed. However, if we are going to continue to use the old label, we had better understand what it no longer means.

Among the things that federalism does *not* mean today are:

1. A constitutionally fixed distribution of functions between the two levels of government;
2. Separation of functions such that there are no overlaps in jurisdiction among the levels of government;

3. Reservation of certain spheres of authority in the states that cannot be touched by the national government;
4. Financial independence on the part of the states;
5. A relationship of coordinate equality between the states and the central government;
6. That the Tenth Amendment provides any obstacle whatsoever to the further extension of the authority of the national government.

Federalism, in short, is not like the Iron Curtain or the Berlin Wall: It is neither something that makes a high barrier between the actions of the national and state governments nor something that has its essence in a competitive relationship. Is there any sense, then, in which federalism remains a constitutional concept? It is not any longer a legal aspect of the system as regards distribution of power between the central and regional governments, for that is now a matter of policy rather than legality, given the breadth of Supreme Court interpretation of the relevant constitutional clauses.

There is, however, one sense in which the constitutional meaning of federalism still has importance. That lies in the guaranteed independent existence of the states. Because the boundaries of a state cannot be changed without its own consent, which is unlikely to be given, even the prescribed formal mechanism for constitutional amendment cannot eliminate a state against its wishes. This fact may not seem very significant, but one of its corollaries is: The fact that the state appoints its own officials. If ours were a unitary state, then at least in theory there is no reason why all civil servants throughout the country might not be appointees of the central government and therefore removable by the government. Under federalism, the jobs of state and local officials derive not from the national but the state capitals, and though the federal government may finance all or part of the salaries of state and local officials and may establish requirements in its grant programs regarding the manner of their appointment, it cannot directly hire or fire them. Because the states do have this one kind of formal autonomy, formal federalism does indirectly maintain a base for local political strength: Since political parties revolve around offices, and states provide offices to be filled by election rather than by national government appointments, constitutional federalism provides a continuing base for some measure of decentralization in the party system. That it requires the present degree of decentralization seems to be doubtful, but we will not go into that. This autonomy of personnel, both elective and appointive, is the remaining significant fact arising out of the constitutional formalities of federalism. All else of the so-called principles of federalism is so much rhetoric today.

The difference between old-style and new-style federalism can be summed up this way: Old-style federalism describes a nonrelationship between the national and state governments, and new-style federalism refers to a maltifaceted positive relationship of shared action. The meaning of federalism today lies in a process of joint action, not in a matter of legal status. It is not a matter of what governments are, but of what they do. It is a matter of action rather than structure. It is dynamic and changing, not static and constant. From the viewpoint of the states and localities, federalism in the form of the politics of intergovernmental relations today amounts to (1) a right to be heard in the design of programs and (2) a right to share in their implementation. If the generic part of the concept of federalism consists of the notion that the parts, as well as the center that represents the whole, have a say in shaping action, then federalism is as alive today as in the time of James Madison.

On the other hand, if one defines federalism this broadly

it becomes almost synonymous with democracy. Why is that? Because in any system that is democratic, whether formally unitary or federalist, the people and their organizations will have an opportunity to be heard, both through the vote and through parliamentary discussion. That is why Great Britain has a long tradition of very vital local government despite its unitary constitutional structure. And, as the Soviet Union illustrates, a country that is not democratic can be ruled arbitrarily from the center despite the clearest kind of constitutional provisions embodying federalism.

What is essential to free government is not formal federalism, but First Amendment freedoms—those of speech, press, and assembly—the right to organize groups and petition the government, and the right to vote. These outlets for whatever pluralism of ideas and interests and values exists in the society constitute the essence of freedom. Institutional patterns do not determine relationships of power but reflect them. That our system of government retains great flexibility in the relationship between the national government and its citizens, and great openness to influence by the citizenry, is easily illustrated when we consider the growth of new modes of local influence, modes that have more than made up for any loss of local strength resulting from the demise of constitutional federalism. The new modes we refer to are *direct federalism* (national-city relationships that bypass state governments) and *private federalism* or *federalism by contract* (relationships by which nongovernmental firms and groups of all kinds perform the government's business under grant or contract). The latter is the essence of what former President Johnson's administration was fond of calling *creative federalism*. Together, direct and private federalism constitute very significant symbols of the liveliness and strength of social forces outside of Washington.

171

PROGNOSIS AND PRESCRIPTION

The Models Revisited

It is time now to take a backward glance at the adequacy of well-known conceptions of federalism in the light of the *Realpolitik* of grants-in-aid and the intergovernmental relations picture that most of this book has been about. The first thing that our analysis does is to back up with the evidence of administrative experience the theoretical formulation popularized by Morton Grodzins under the label of *marble cake federalism*. While not by any means the only way in which the federal government shares functions and authority with the state and local governments, grants-in-aid are certainly "where the action is" today. The quality of federalism (in the sense of sharing power between central and regional jurisdictions) is, we think, much more vitally affected by sharing that involves intimate day-by-day association, as do all grants-in-aid but particularly project grants, than by those instances of sharing that are discrete and discontinuous, such as the simultaneous existence of both federal and state legislation affecting elections or the party system or the sporadic connections involved in federal court review of state court judgments.

At the same time, however, Grodzins perhaps carried the implications of his analogy further than was justified. In his various writings on federalism, including his posthumous book *The American System*, there is an implication that proof that the states were involved in activities jointly with the national government proved also the continuing vitality and strength of state vis-à-vis national government. That is to say, he may to some extent have confused sharing of functions with sharing of power. Because he was very much a pluralist (a believer that the national interest could be defined as the action that resulted from the free interplay of competing groups), he stressed as a matter of value as well as of fact the force of localism in the American party system and at least implicitly suggested that this force would keep the national government from dominating the marble cake. Grodzins's book was published in 1966, and the editing had been finished the previous summer. He died in 1964, just before the explosive proliferation of grant programs, particularly those of a project nature with fairly tight requirements for federal approval. Grodzins's conception of sharing still holds up as a major corrective to the older image of dual federalism, with its pretense that national government stays out of most domestic areas that state and local governments are engaged in. It is, however, an inadequate conception as regards the delineation of the intergovernmental relationship in terms of the thrust of power and the answer to the question: Who decides what the priorities will be?

Both the dual federalism conception and the extremely legalistic and formal criteria for testing the presence of federalism set forth by K. C. Wheare can be rejected as pictures of the American intergovernmental system. *Dual federalism*, the reader may recall, was the term used by the late Edward S. Corwin to capture the flavor of the late nineteenth- and early twentieth-century period in which the Supreme Court interpreted the American Constitution as requiring a hands-off relationship between state and national governments. The national government was not to regulate many matters—such as child labor or industrial safety—because these were presumed to lie within the area of jurisdiction reserved to the states or to the people by the Tenth Amendment and were not (as later came to be the case) considered open to national action on the basis of a broad interpretation of the commerce clause. The states, meanwhile, were for a time forbidden to act in the same areas on the grounds that to do so was to take property without due process or to interfere with liberty of contract. That kind of federalism created a no-man's-land in which neither level of government could act, let alone think about joint action. Wheare's litmus test for federalism includes a requirement that the regional governments be financially independent of the central government, which we have clearly seen that they are not; he also requires that the power relationship be such as to justify the adjective *coordinate,* as distinguished from superordinate and subordinate. As we remarked at the outset, that is not the case.

Ever since the constitutional revolution of 1937, the nation-state relationship has been seen as predominantly one of *cooperative federalism.* This means, at the least, that where the national government has not acted, the states are generally free to act, so that we are not without government at all in some areas, as was the case for a time under dual federalism. And at the most, cooperative federalism means something close to the marble cake conception of simultaneous national and state action in the same sphere. So far as it goes, cooperative federalism is still an accurate enough label, as was the Johnsonian sequel, *creative federalism,* as a shorthand way of referring to the development of administrative relationships in which the national government uses nongovernmental bodies as administrative entities to carry out its programs. Neither of these concepts, however, says anything about the question of who dominates in a partnership or cooperative arrangement.

Beginning in 1969, President Nixon proselytized for the phrase *New Federalism,* by which was meant a purposeful movement toward state-local dominance in the partnerships of our time. As we have seen, the essence of this concept lay in reviving the days when there were no national priorities, when there was no particular content to the concept of national citizenship, and when to speak of one's "community" usually meant one's home town, but never the United States as an integrated national entity. The Nixonian New Federalism was simply romantic rhetoric, a facade behind which the national government is to abrogate its domestic role, to reduce its presence merely to that of an onlooker—or a fairy godmother who will provide the wherewithal for Cinderella in the form of state and local governments to achieve her wishes.

We propose a new label. (We might as well play the game too.) Ours is *permissive federalism.* That phrase conveys the notion that there is a sharing of power and authority between the national and state governments, but that the state's share rests upon the permission and permissiveness of the national government. The broadness or specificity of congressional grant legislation measures in each instance the degree of national consensus versus state and local diversity that exists with regard to the subject matter of that particular legislation. The national government unquestionably possesses the legal authority to impose whatever degree of restrictiveness it wishes. It should be clear at once that this is not federalism at all in the classic conception. Federalism in that sense is dead. We have at least become one nation, indivisible, and if justice for all is to be achieved, it will not be by leaving its definition to the dominant factions of small areas. James Madison was, after all, right: The larger the area and diversity of populations encompassed in a governmental jurisdiction, the less the chance that any one faction will ride roughshod over others. We were, however, too diverse and socially pluralistic for a long time to permit the results even of pluralistic politics to produce national action. We have now achieved that degree of unity and can express a national consensus that does not represent the final victory of any one elite or any one interest, but the embodiment of difficult-to-arrive-at coalition agreements.

Is Permissive Federalism Good?

To state that the system is one of permissive federalism is to state a fact and not an evaluation. Is it a good thing, or something to be regretted? That is our final question. We think the careful reader of the preceding pages will know our answer: In our opinion, a system of shared functions and shared power under federal leadership and within the boundaries set by whatever priorities a national consensus is able to agree upon is very much the right thing. We no longer need the constitutional pluralism of the dual federalism type. Granted that there are still some regional diversities and perhaps even differences in state cultures, these can be sufficiently accommodated within the boundaries of implementation of permissive federalism; they do not require the abstention of the national government from domestic affairs. Actually, James Madison was almost too right in his prediction that government in the larger area would prevent domination by a single interest: It almost prevents any resolution at all of a public interest. Our problem may not be that the national government has become too powerful while state and local government are weak and atrophied; it may be instead that the national government is only now beginning to achieve the amount of power needed to govern effectively.

At least one political scientist has argued that the national government has allowed far too much of its own programs to be shaped by unaccountable local governments and local nongovernmental groups. Theodore J. Lowi, in *The End of Liberalism,* attacks what he calls "interest-group liberalism" as a vulgarization of pluralism that "renders government impotent." In this view, "liberal leaders do not wield the authority of democratic government with the resoluteness of men certain of the legitimacy of their positions, the integrity of their institutions, or the justness of the programs they serve."[6]

Lowi discusses at some length the war on poverty of the Johnson administration and argues that the Economic Opportunity Act of 1964 represented a total abnegation of the federal government's responsibilities because it failed to define a conception of poverty; it failed to define a methodology for attacking poverty; and in its most innovative feature, that of the Community Action Programs, it was simply an open-ended invitation for local groups to define their own policy regarding poverty. The Community Action Programs, he argues, were completely "process-oriented" and lacked all substantive guidance for either the head administrators in Washington or the local grant-receiving groups in the cities. According to Lowi, interest group liberalism, which is the dominant political ideology of the United States at the present time, insists upon overdoing the notion of representation at points where it is inappropriate. That is, it confuses representation with administration, and in so doing makes it impossible for government to give firm definition to policy at the top. To provide representation down at the bottom is to let policy be made at the bottom. In his view, this is decentralization run riot: "A time when national standards and local realities are almost completely out of joint is hardly a time for decentralization."[7]

It is undoubtedly true that delegation of program-defining and to some extent policy-defining power to local groups occasionally means that the shape of local initiatives will be contrary to national policy, as in the instance of a southern city's plans for segregated urban renewal, which were once accepted by a federal agency. At other times, the locally initiated programs will simply be ineffective and a waste of money. But it is also true that on still other occasions, good ideas will be brought forward which might not have occurred to the program leadership in Washington. Innovation is hard to come by in public policy, and it is worth some risk and some price in misdirected or ineffective efforts. Regardless of whether or not one agrees with Lowi's evaluation, however, it is hard to argue with his analysis of the situation. He provides very good evidence and argument in support of his proposition that policy making in many of the newer domestic programs is already very heavily decentralized because of the present passion for participatory democracy in the administration of programs. And if Lowi is correct, then former President Nixon and many other devotees of revenue sharing are not correct as regards the present balance between national and state-local power.

Permissive federalism is good, we conclude, exactly because it can strengthen the national government by permitting firm national definitions of policy objectives and program approaches at the same time that it can make all the room needed for appropriate state-local inputs to the details of program implementation. Permissive federalism is, in fact, the effective key to administrative decentralization because such decentralization makes sense and provides accountability only when it is within the boundaries and constraints set by firmly developed policy at the top. Dual federalism was wrong because it encouraged a false competition between state and national governments and left too many problems in a no-man's-land in between. Cooperative federalism was an improvement because it presumed that there would always be room for some government to act, and it encouraged the levels to act jointly on occasion. But it was inadequate conceptually because it assumed that the responsibilities of state and national governments were co-ordinate, whereas in reality the national government needs to be superior. Its cooperation with the states should always be on the basis of national standards; it should not adjust its scales to state-local standards, which in many instances would be below its own.

Permissive federalism in the eighties may be more flexible than in the seventies because the block grant approach experimented with in CETA and CDBG gives us an alternative tool to that of categorical grants, another way of combining national agenda setting and broad targeting but without abnegating national responsibility, as New Federalism in its original sense would have done. The newest federalism (let's leave it lower case) will be a mixture of blocks and categoricals, of formula and project grants, but all within the context of permissive federalism. General revenue sharing may survive as a mode of quite limited unfettered income transfer to subnational governments, but it will not supplant the grant-in-aid system that has so successfully mushroomed and matured in the past two decades as an effective marriage of national policy making and local operations. The mixed system we have may not be tidy; but it works.

Notes

1 IS FEDERALISM DEAD?

1. William H. Riker, *Federalism* (Boston: Little, Brown, 1964).
2. Grodzins's major work, which was posthumous and edited by Daniel J. Elazar, is *The American System* (Chicago: Rand, McNally, 1966); Daniel J. Elazar, *The American Partnership* (Chicago: Rand, McNally, 1962).
3. Morton Grodzins, "The Federal System," in President's Commission on National Goals, *Goals for Americans* (Englewood Cliffs, N.J.: Prentice-Hall, 1960).
4. K. C. Wheare, *Federal Government*, 3rd ed. (New York: Oxford University Press, 1953), pp. 11, 2, and Chapter I generally.
5. Ibid, p. 53.
6. *U.S.* v. *Darby*, 312 U.S. 100, 1941.
7. *U.S.* v. *Butler*, 297 U.S. 1.
8. M. J. C. Vile, *The Structure of American Federalism* (New York: Oxford University Press, 1961), pp. 3, 65.
9. David B. Walker, "A New Intergovernmental System in 1977," *Publius* 8 (Winter 1978):104.
10. William Anderson, *The Nation and the States* (Minneapolis: University of Minnesota Press, 1955), pp. 135–36.
11. Thomas Dye and L. Harmon Zeigler, *The Irony of Democracy*, 3rd ed. (Belmont, Calif.: Duxbury Press, 1975), pp. 388–89.
12. David J. Olson and Philip Meyer, *Governing the United States*, 2nd ed. (New York: McGraw-Hill, 1978), p. 41.
13. Ira Carmen, *Power and Balance* (New York: Harcourt, Brace, Jovanovich, 1978), pp. 346, 387.
14. James M. Burns et al., *Government by the People*, 10th ed. (Englewood Cliffs, N.J.: Prentice-Hall, 1978), pp. 48, 59, 62.
15. Kenneth Prewitt and Sidney Verba, *An Introduction to American Government* (New York: Harper & Row, 1977), pp. 434–35.

16. Robert K. Carr et al., *Essentials of American Democracy*, 7th ed. (Hinsdale, Ill.: Dryden Press, 1974), pp.130, 132–33.
17. Peter K. Eisinger et al., *American Politics: The People and the Polity* (Boston: Little, Brown, 1978), p. 52.
18. Theodore L. Becker, *American Government: Past, Present, Future* (Boston: Allyn and Bacon, 1976), p. 110.
19. Dan Nimmo and Thomas Ungs, *Political Patterns in America* (San Francisco: W. H. Freeman, 1979), p. 60.
20. On dual federalism generally, see Edward S. Corwin, *The Twilight of the Supreme Court* (New Haven: Yale University Press, 1934), ch. 1.
21. 247 U.S. 251 (1918).
22. 96 Supreme Court 2465; 426 U.S. 833.
23. See Theodore J. Lowi, *The End of Liberalism* (New York: Norton, 1969).
24. Quoted in Aaron Wildavsky, ed., *American Federalism in Perspective* (Boston: Little, Brown, 1967), pp. 37, 36.
25. Both arguments may be found in Wildavsky, ibid.
26. Vile, *Structure of American Federalism*, p. 39.

2 THE CRISIS OF FISCAL FEDERALISM

1. Walter W. Heller, *New Dimensions of Political Economy* (Cambridge, Mass.: Harvard University Press, 1967), p.129.
2. Ibid., pp. 121–22.
3. J. K. Galbraith, *The Affluent Society* (Boston: Houghton Mifflin, 1958), p. 263.
4. Fiscal and other statistics cited in this book are to be found, for the most part, in the *Special Analysis* series of the U.S. Office of Management and Budget; *Statistical Abstracts of the United States*, various editions; or the monographic publications of the U.S. Advisory Commission on Intergovernmental Relations.
5. L. L. Ecker-Racz, *The Politics and Economics of State-Local Finance* (Englewood Cliffs, N.J.: Prentice-Hall, 1970), p. 39.
6. Henry S. Reuss, *Revenue Sharing* (New York: Praeger, 1970), p. 27.
7. Ibid., p. 26.
8. Ecker-Racz, *State-Local Finance*, pp. 202, 77.

9. Ibid., p. 210.
10. Ibid., p. 20.

3 *GRANTS-IN-AID: THE CUTTING EDGE OF INTERGOVERNMENTAL RELATIONS*

1. Quoted in William H. Young, *Ogg and Ray's Introduction to American Government* (New York: Appleton, 1966), p. 62.
2. For an excellent descriptive history of the development of grants-in-aid, see W. Brooks Graves, *Intergovernmental Relations in the United States* (New York: Scribner's, 1964), chapters 14–16.
3. Letter to author from Samuel L. Becker, acting director, Division of Mental Health Service Programs, National Institute of Mental Health, U.S. Department of Health, Education and Welfare, August 18, 1971.
4. Graves, *Intergovermental Relations*, p. 546.
5. E. E. Schattschneider, *The Semi-Sovereign People* (New York: Holt, Rinehart & Winston, 1961).
6. For a relatively brief yet authoritative presentation of the external-benefits justification for grants-in-aid, see George F. Break, *Intergovernmental Fiscal Relations* (Washington, D.C.: The Brookings Institution, 1967), chapter 3.
7. National Science Board, *Toward a Public Policy for Graduate Education in Sciences* (Washington, D.C.: National Science Foundation, 1968), pp. 37–38.
8. Phillip Monypenny, "Federal Grants-in-Aid to State Governments: A Political Analysis," *National Tax Journal* 13 (March 1960):1–16.
9. Advisory Commission on Intergovernmental Relations, *Fiscal Balance in the American Federal System*, (Washington, D.C.: ACIR, 1957), I, 149.
10. James L. Sundquist, *Making Federalism Work* (Washington, D.C.: The Brookings Institute, 1969), p. 127.
11. Commission on Intergovernmental Relations, *Report* (Washington, D.C.: Government Publishing Office, 1955), p. 64.
12. These quotations and the discussion in which they are embedded are found in Sundquist, *Making Federalism Work*, pp. 3–6.

13. Walter Lippman, *The Public Philosophy* (London: Hamish Hamilton, 1955), p. 44.
14. Break, *Intergovernmental Fiscal Relations,* p. 95.
15. ACIR, *Fiscal Balance,* I, 153.

4 REVENUE SHARING: A CASE OF ARRESTED DEVELOPMENT

1. PL. 92–513, October 20, 1972.
2. State of the Union message delivered before the 92nd Congress, January 1971.
3. See George Sternlieb and James W. Hughes, "New Regional and Metropolitan Realities in America," *Journal of the American Institute of Planners* 43, No. 3 (1977):227–41; their *Post-Industrial America: Metropolitan Decline and Inter-Regional Job Shifts* (Rutgers, N.J.: The Center for Urban Policy Research, 1978); and studies prepared by the Northeast-Midwest Congressional Coalition.
4. See Jeffrey Pressman and Aaron Wildavsky, *Implementation* (Berkeley: University of California Press, 1973).
5. Jeffrey Pressman, *Federal Programs and City Politics* (Berkeley: University of California Press, 1975).
6. For example, see *Publius: The Journal of Federalism;* the publications of the Center for the Study of Federalism at Temple University; and in general the writings of Deil Wright, David Walker, Catherine Lovell, David Porter, and Vincent Ostrom. In particular, Daniel J. Elazar, *American Federalism: A View From the States* (New York: Crowell, 1972) should be consulted.
7. For example, see Vincent Ostrom, *The Intellectual Crisis of American Public Administration* (Auburn, Ala.: The University of Alabama Press, 1973); and Robert Bish and Vincent Ostrom, *Understanding Urban Government* (Washington, D.C.: American Enterprise Institute, 1973). *The Public Interest* also reflects this position.
8. "There Are Surpluses in the Statehouses—But Can They Last Forever?" *National Journal,* January 21, 1978, p. 98.
9. Ibid., p. 95.
10. Ibid.

11. Melville J. Ulmer, "The Limitations of Revenue Sharing," *Annals* of the American Academy of Political and Social Science 397 (September 1971): 48–59.
12. "Mass Truce Over Highway Funds," *National Journal,* November 19, 1977, p. 1812.
13. See Elazar, *American Federalism.*
14. Quoted in Charles Adrian, *State and Local Governments,* 4th ed. (New York: McGraw-Hill, 1976), p. 56.
15. Daniel R. Grant, "Urban Needs and State Response: Local Government Re-Organization," in A. K. Campbell, ed., *The States and the Urban Crisis* (Englewood Cliffs, N.J.: Prentice-Hall, 1970), p. 111.
16. Adrian, *State and Local Government.*
17. "State and Local Governments Struggle to Make Ends Meet," *National Journal,* September 18, 1976, p. 1321.
18. See "Some States Are Putting Their Urban Strategies to Work," *National Journal,* October 15, 1977, pp. 1605–07.
19. Ibid.
20. Ibid.
21. Cited in "State and Local Governments Struggle to Make Ends Meet."
22. See Alice Rivlin, *Systematic Thinking for Social Action* (Washington, D.C.: The Brookings Institution, 1971).
23. Parris Glendening and Mavis Mann Reeves, *Pragmatic Federalism: An Intergovernmental View of American Government* (Palisades, Calif.: Palisades Publishers, 1977), pp. 65–66.
24. See National Science Foundation, *General Revenue Sharing,* III, "Synthesis of Formula Research" (October 1975), chapter 3 for a detailed analysis of the formula issues.
25. Richard Nathan and Charles Adams, Jr., and associates, *Revenue Sharing: The Second Round* (Washington, D.C.: The Brookings Institution, 1977), p. 107.
26. See National Science Foundation, *General Revenue Sharing,* IV, "Synthesis of Impact and Process Research" (December 1975), chapter 5, p. 17.
27. Quoted in Nathan et al., *Revenue Sharing: The Second Round,* p. 170.
28. National Science Foundation, "Synthesis of Formula Research," p. 1.

29. Deil S. Wright, "State Finances and the Allocation of State General Revenue Sharing Dollars," in Walter F. Scheffer, ed., *General Revenue Sharing and Decentralization* (Norman, Okla.: University of Oklahoma Press, 1975), p. 175.

30. Richard Nathan et al., *Monitoring Revenue Sharing* (Washington, D.C.: The Brookings Institution, 1975), and Nathan et al., *Revenue Sharing: The Second Round.* See also the National Science Foundation, *General Revneue Sharing: Research Utilization Project,* 5 vols. (Washington, D.C., 1975), I, "Summaries of Formula Research" (July 1975); II, "Summaries of Impact and Process Research" (August 1975); III, "Synthesis of Formula Research" (October 1975); IV, "Synthesis of Impact and Process Research" (December 1975); V, "Ancilla to Revenue Sharing Research" (December 1975).

31. National Science Foundation, "Synthesis of Impact and Process Research," p. 59.

32. Ibid.

33. Nathan et al., *Revenue Sharing: The Second Round,* pp. 112–13.

34. Ibid., p. 131.

35. See ibid., p. 164.

36. Ibid., pp. 133–34.

37. On the 20-percent formula issue, see ibid., p. 145.

38. Ibid., p. 42.

39. Jeffrey L. Pressman, "The Political Implications of the New Federalism," in Wallace E. Oates, ed., *Financing the New Federalism* (Washington, D.C.: Resources for the Future, 1975), p. 37.

40. Sarah F. Liebschutz, "General Revenue Sharing as a Political Resource for Local Officials," in C. O. Jones and R. D. Thomas, eds., *Public Policy Making in a Federal System* (Beverly Hills, Calif.:) Sage Publications, 1976), p. 122.

41. Nathan et al., *Revenue Sharing: The Second Round,* pp. 70–71.

42. Ibid., p. 71.

43. See Paul Terrell, *The Social Impact of Revenue Sharing* (New York: Praeger, 1976) for a study of seven atypical recipient governments that supported social services far above the national average.

44. See Nathan et al., *Revenue Sharing: The Second Round,* for an analysis of criticisms of the civil rights provisions.

5 *BLOCK GRANTS: A MIDDLE WAY*

1. Advisory Commission on Intergovernmental Relations, *Block Grants: A Comparative Analysis* (Washington, D.C.: ACIR No. A–60, 1977), p. 45. Cited hereafter as ACIR A–60.
2. Advisory Commission on Intergovernmental Relations, *Categorical Grants: Their Role and Design* (Washington, D.C.: ACIR No. A–52, 1977), p. 25.
3. Based upon a description in Robert P. Inman et al., *Financing the New Federalism* (Baltimore: Johns Hopkins University Press, 1975), pp. 28–32.
4. ACIR A–60, pp. 20, 26.
5. Advisory Commission on Intergovernmental Relations, *Summary and Conclusions: The Intergovernmental Grant System* (Washington, D.C.: ACIR No. A–62, 1978), p. 24.
6. William Mirengoff and Lester Rindler, *CETA: Manpower Programs Under Local Control* (Washington, D.C.: National Academy of Sciences–National Research Council, 1978), p. 12.
7. Ibid., p. 13.
8. Ibid., pp. 86–88.
9. Ibid., p. 271.
10. The reader should consult the three major studies of the CDBG experience, all published by the Department of Housing and Urban Development, Washington, D.C.: Richard P. Nathan et al., *Block Grants for Community Development* (January 1977); Nathan et al., *Decentralizing Community Development* (June 1978); and Paul Dommel et al., *Targeting Community Development* (November 1979).
11. Nathan et al., *Block Grants for Community Development*, p. 499.
12. Ibid., p. 498.
13. U.S. General Accounting Office, *Management and Evaluation of the Community Development Block Grant Program Need To Be Strengthened* (Washington, D.C.: USGA, August 1978), p. 3.
14. Advisory Commission on Intergovernmental Relations, *State Community Assistance Initiatives: Innovations of the Late 70's* (Washington, D.C.: ACIR, May 1979), pp. 1–2.
15. ACIR A–60, p. 42.
16. Ibid., pp. 21–25.

6 IN PRAISE OF PERMISSIVE FEDERALISM

1. Chester I. Barnard, *The Functions of the Executive* (Cambridge, Mass.: Harvard University Press, 1938).
2. Morton Grodzins, *The American System*, edited by Daniel J. Elazar (Chicago: Rand, McNally, 1962), pp. 376–78.
3. Martha Derthick, *The Influence of Federal Grants* (Cambridge, Mass.: Harvard University Press, 1970), p. 196.
4. Ibid., p. 195.
5. Ibid.
6. Theodore J. Lowi, *The End of Liberalism* (New York: Norton, 1969), p. 288.
7. Ibid., pp. 226–39, 268.

Bibliography

Advisory Commission on Intergovernmental Relations. *The Intergovernmental Grant System: An Assessment and Proposed Policies.* A series of 14 volumes published between October 1976 and June 1978. Washington, D.C.: Advisory Commission on Intergovernmental Relations, 1976–78.

Break, George F. *Intergovernmental Fiscal Relations in the United States.* Washington, D.C.: The Brookings Institution, 1967.

Caputo, David, special ed. *General Revenue Sharing and Federalism. Annals* of the American Academy of Political and Social Science 419 (May 1975).

Caputo, David A., and Cole, Richard L. *Urban Politics and Decentralization: The Case of General Revenue Sharing.* Lexington, Mass.: Lexington Books, 1974.

Davis, S. Rufus. *The Federal Principle.* Berkeley, Calif.: University of California Press, 1978.

Derthick, Martha. *Between State and Nation.* Washington, D.C.: The Brookings Institution, 1974.

————. *The Influence of Federal Grants.* Cambridge, Mass.: Harvard University Press, 1970.

Dommel, Paul K. *The Politics of Revenue Sharing.* Bloomington, Ind.: University of Indiana Press, 1974.

Duchacek, Ivo D. *Comparative Federalism*. New York: Holt, Rinehart and Winston, 1970.

Ecker-Racz, L. L. *The Politics and Economics of State-Local Finance*. Englewood Cliffs, N.J.: Prentice Hall, 1970.

Elazar, Daniel J. *American Federalism: A View from the States*. 2nd ed. New York: Crowell, 1972.

Feld, Richard D., and Grafton, Carl, eds. *The Uneasy Partnership: The Dynamics of Federal, State and Urban Relations*. Palo Alto, Calif.: National Press Books, 1973.

Frieden, Bernard J., and Kaplan, Marshall. *The Politics of Neglect: Urban Aid from Model Cities to Revenue Sharing*. Cambridge, Mass.: M.I.T. Press, 1975.

Gelfand, Mark I. *A Nation of Cities: The Federal Government and Urban America 1933–1965*. New York: Oxford University Press, 1975.

Glendening, Parris N., and Reeves, Mavis Mann. *Pragmatic Federalism*. Palisades, Calif.: Palisades Publishers, 1977.

Graves, W. Brooks. *Intergovernmental Relations*. New York: Scribner's, 1964.

Grodzins, Morton. *The American System*. Edited by Daniel J. Elazar. Chicago: Rand, McNally, 1966.

Harbert, Anita S. *Federal Grants-In-Aid*. New York: Praeger, 1976.

Heller, Walter W. *New Dimensions of Political Economy*. Cambridge, Mass.: Harvard University Press, 1967.

Hubbell, L. Kenneth, ed. *Fiscal Crisis in American Cities: The Federal Response*. Cambridge, Mass.: Ballinger, 1979.

Inman, Robert P., et al. *Financing the New Federalism*. Baltimore: Johns Hopkins University Press, for Resources for the Future, 1975.

Intergovernmental Perspective. A quarterly journal of factual information regarding current developments and short policy evaluation articles. Published by Advisory Commission on Intergovernmental Relations. Vols. 4–6, 1978–1980.

Jones, Charles O., and Thomas, Robert D., eds. *Public Policy Making in a Federal System*. Beverly Hills, Calif.: Sage, 1976.

Larkey, Patrick D. *Evaluating Public Programs: The Impact of General Revenue Sharing on Municipal Government.* Princeton, N.J.: Princeton University Press, 1979.

Leach, Richard. *American Federalism.* New York: W. W. Norton, 1970.

MacMahon, Arthur W. *Administering Federalism in A Democracy.* New York: Oxford University Press, 1972.

Martin, Roscoe. *The Cities and the Federal System.* New York: Atherton Press, 1965.

Maxwell, James A., and Aronson, J. Richard. *Financing State and Local Governments.* 3rd ed. Washington, D.C.: The Brookings Institution, 1977.

Mirengoff, William, and Rindler, Lester. *CETA: Manpower Programs Under Local Control.* Washington, D.C.: National Academy of Sciences–National Research Council, 1978.

Nathan, Richard P., et al. *Monitoring Revenue Sharing.* Washington, D.C.: The Brookings Institution, 1975.

————. *Revenue Sharing: The Second Round.* Washington, D.C.: The Brookings Institution, 1977.

Oates, Wallace E. *Fiscal Federalism.* New York: Harcourt, Brace, Jovanovich, 1972.

Reuss, Henry. *Revenue Sharing: Crutch or Catalyst for State and Local Governments.* New York: Praeger, 1970.

Riker, William H. *Federalism.* Boston: Little, Brown, 1964.

Sharkansky, Ira. *The Maligned States.* 2nd ed. New York: McGraw-Hill, 1978.

Sundquist, James L. *Making Federalism Work.* Washington, D.C.: The Brookings Institution, 1969.

Terrell, Paul, with the assistance of Stan Weisner. *The Social Impact of Revenue Sharing.* New York: Praeger, 1976.

Walker, David B. "A New Intergovernmental System in 1977." *Publius* 8 (Winter 1978):101–16.

Wheare, K. C. *Federal Government.* 3rd ed. New York: Oxford University Press, 1953.

Wildavsky, Aaron, ed. *American Federalism in Perspective.* Boston: Little, Brown, 1967.

Wright, Deil S. *Understanding Intergovernmental Relations.* North Scituate, Mass.: Duxbury Press, 1978.

Index